Auntie Mabel's War

AN ACCOUNT OF HER PART IN THE HOSTILITIES OF 1914–18

COMPILED BY MARIAN WENZEL AND JOHN CORNISH

ALLEN LANE

ALLEN LANE

Penguin Books Ltd

536 King's Road

London SW10 0UH

First published 1980

Copyright © Marian Wenzel and John Cornish, 1980

ISBN 0 7139 1265 0

Set in Monophoto Baskerville
Printed in Great Britain by
Butler & Tanner Ltd, Frome and London

CONTENTS

INTRODUCTION   6

1   PROLOGUE: CONCERNING AN OBJECT: MRS. TURNER IS REMINDED OF HER AUNTIE MABEL   8

2   THE PRE-WAR YEARS: SHEFFIELD AND ENVIRONS, HOME OF THE BRAVE   10

3   1914: IN THE SUMMER OF WHICH THE PEACE OF EUROPE IS DISRUPTED BY THE OUTBREAK OF A DREADFUL WAR...   20

4   1915: AUNTIE MABEL VOLUNTEERS...   24

5   1916: THE WAR CONTINUES, BUT MUST SOON BE OVER   52

6   1917: THE WAR *STILL* CONTINUES: BUT MUST SOON BE OVER   76

7   1918: IN WHICH THE WAR *FINALLY* ENDS   91

8   AFTER THE WAR: MOPPING UP EUROPE; MABEL LENDS A HAND   106

9   EPILOGUE: CONCERNING SOME MORE OBJECTS; MRS. TURNER RESUMES HER NARRATIVE: SHE PONDERS AUNTIE MABEL'S WAR TROPHIES   121

Mabel Jeffery, the heroine of this book, was the aunt of my friend Mrs. Turner on the Isle of Man, who lives in a house with a great feeling of family history. I learned about this aunt gradually. On a visit to Mrs. Turner a few years ago I was, as is my custom, making drawings of things around the house and noting down in Mrs. Turner's own words the family stories about them. Our attention turned to some relics of the 1914–18 war – shell cases with punchwork flowers and so on, the sort of thing which could be seen in half the houses in Britain a generation or two ago – and I heard for the first time about Mrs. Turner's Auntie Mabel, who had been a nurse in France and the Balkans during and after the war, and who had brought home the objects in question.

A memento box was produced which contained Mabel's literary remains, as it were: the postcards she sent home to her family, her note-books and jottings. It also contained letters written to her by grateful patients, various official forms relating to her movements, and some family photographs.

I was at first attracted by the somewhat whimsical impression of those now far-off days that these remains conveyed – the horrific picture post-cards inscribed on the reverse with enquiries as to holidays in Blackpool – but I became increasingly involved with the character of Mabel herself that emerged. I decided to put together a book with the collaboration of John Cornish – a book which would introduce the reader to Auntie Mabel as I had met her myself: first in the words of Mrs. Turner, and then in her own words and those of her friends, unfolding the progress of the Great War as it appeared to them.

Thus the middle of the book, Chapters 3 to 8, presents the story mostly in the words of Mabel and her correspondents, items in other languages being translated into English; while the beginning and end, Chapters 1, 2 and 9, contain what Mrs. Turner remembers about Auntie Mabel and her life as the family knew and told it. That these two pictures do not always correspond is part of the point. People willingly go to suffer horrors of war in the conviction that by so doing they protect those left at home from greater horrors. They often succeed to the extent of obscuring from those protected just what was endured for their sakes; and this can be true of nurses as well as soldiers. So Mrs. Turner's narrative is not used as a frame simply for "artistic" reasons; it is part of what Auntie Mabel and all the others were fighting to preserve.

Mabel's poetry notebooks, to which she added throughout her life, con-tain the following entry for the war years:

"And methought that beauty and terror were only one, not two,
And the world has room for love and death, and thunder and dew,
And all the sinews of hell slumber in summer air,
And the face of God is a rock, but the face of the rock is fair."
(*Robert Louis Stevenson*)

One wonders how often these sentiments were shared by other heroic women who went to do their bit.

Marian Wenzel

ACKNOWLEDGEMENTS

Firstly of course thanks are due to Mrs. Turner for loaning us the materials for this book, and for permission to reproduce them. On matters of military and nursing history we have much appreciated help from T. C. Charman of the Imperial War Museum, Paul J. Eyre, Director of the City of London Sector of the London Branch, British Red Cross Society, and Mrs. Joy Fawcett, Archivist of the British Red Cross Society Archives at Guildford. We have received further help and advice from Alice Wordie and Mrs. J. M. Cregeen, J.P., of the Stirling Red Cross Headquarters. Lewis Jillings of the University of Stirling helped with the German material as mentioned below. Finally we should like to thank our editor, Geraldine Cooke, who encouraged us to make this book.

THE TRANSLATIONS

Translations from German and French material appear in this book. The German items consist of notes on the backs of postcards discovered in the pocket of a dead German officer (pp. 86, 87). Lewis Jillings found these inscriptions grammatical and easy to translate once he was victorious in his heroic battle with the script, which to the eye of any but one well versed in German handwriting styles of the period was quite indecipherable. The French items, mainly communications from Mabel's French patients, colleagues and friends, appear throughout the book. John Cornish translated these, and had less trouble than Lewis Jillings with the scripts, which were easily legible, but more trouble with sense. Many of Mabel's soldier-correspondents were barely literate, so translation had to be carried out on a phonetic basis which allowed "*mais*" to stand for "*mes*", "*vaux*" for "*vos*", "*ses*" for "*c'est*", and so on. We felt that a reasonable degree of sense indicated a reasonable degree of success, though a few obscurities remain. John Cornish also wishes to accept the full blame for the English doggerel renderings of the "poetic" bits of French. Translations from Serbian printed material are by Marian Wenzel.

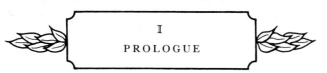
CONCERNING AN OBJECT:
MRS. TURNER IS REMINDED OF HER AUNTIE MABEL

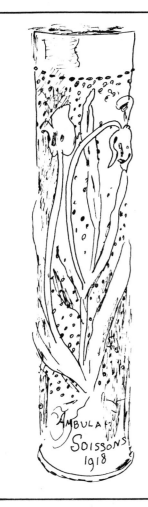

Yes, that thing by the fireplace with the flowers on it is really a shell case. It's from the First World War. My mother's only sister, my Auntie Mabel,[1] was my only blood auntie, and it was something she got. She trained as a nurse before the First World War, and then she joined the Red Cross. So she was fully qualified before the First World War broke out. She went to France and said it was terrible; sometimes she had only six hours to evacuate a whole hospital. Her name was the same as my mother's maiden name, Jeffery. Well, Mother said when the First World War started and she joined the work Mabel had black hair, but when it was over she was white. They were always chased from pillar to post.

She brought that back from France for her parents; I thought it was an awfully morbid thing. They had enough trouble over here. But they were all pure brass, and some bright soul as soon as the war was over saw his chance. I suppose they were lying all over the battlefields. It has a date of 1918 and the name of Soissons. That was where it was found, and where she got it to bring back. I could have thought of nicer things to bring back. But I guess it was all the rage. It got to Granny's house and then it came here. I think it's morbid, even with the sort of embroidered design on it. If it had been me I'd have put it under the hydrangeas. I often look at it and wonder how many men its shell killed.

1. Mabel Effie Jeffery, 1883–1958.

Somewhere around there's all her photographs, and a memento box with the postcards
she wrote back to her family from the war. Let's see if we can find them.

That's Auntie Mabel with the rest of her family, as a young girl, peeping through a gate. She seems a bit prim even then. Grandpa, Mabel's father, was quite an amateur photographer; he used big plates and Mother said he used to run and get himself in the picture.

Too bad! Mabel must have torn something out here.

Harry was her only brother, eldest of the family, and there he is in cricket kit, with Auntie Mabel sat on the ground. My mother's on the swing. Don't they look cute! Victorian youth.

So here they all are together. That's Grandpa and Grandma, and Auntie Mabel down on the bottom sitting, and Uncle Harry standing next to his fiancée, Adeline. And that's my mum, Maud, next to Mabel. Isn't she a poppet!

They are in the garden of the home my Grandmother and Grandpa had at Deepcar, Sheffield. That's where the family was brought up. It was very near Stocksbridge, where my Grandpa's, I think, great-uncle started this sort of steel production, called Fox's. The whole valley was given over to it really. They had railway lines bringing over the raw materials. Sheffield in those days was full of blast furnaces.

Fox's started out making crinoline frames. Then they evolved into umbrella frames when Mother and Auntie Mabel were around; Fox's umbrella frames were quite famous. Samuel Fox was the original founder of the firm, and I believe his sons were rather uninterested, and somehow it passed to Grandpa and his brother.

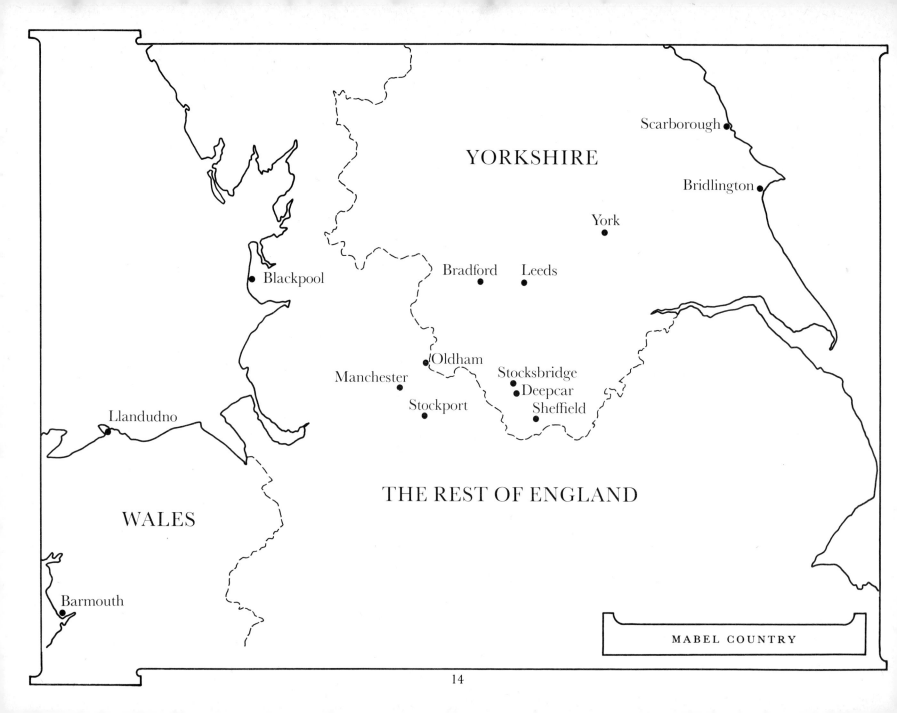

YORKSHIRE

Scarborough

Bridlington

York

Bradford   Leeds

Blackpool

Oldham

Stocksbridge

Manchester

Deepcar

Stockport

Sheffield

THE REST OF ENGLAND

Llandudno

WALES

Barmouth

MABEL COUNTRY

You know that imitation fox in the hall? Well he was a trade mascot for the Fox's Stocksbridge works. He always used to sit in my grandfather's vestibule hall. I was allowed to play with him for a limited time but I was *never* allowed to take him to bed; he was very special to Grandpa. I used to kiss his nose and stroke him down and I used to call him Teddy Fox, but my golly, Teddy Fox had to be treated with respect.

And when he came to me Auntie Mabel had been using him for – you know how in the beginning of the century hatpin things were great? They were for those real Edwardian flower garden hats like Mabel is wearing in that small photo I have. Well, Teddy Fox was all stuck with hatpins, and there were feathers stuck in his tail. Fancy doing that to him. I removed all the nasty hatpins, but the feathers I left.

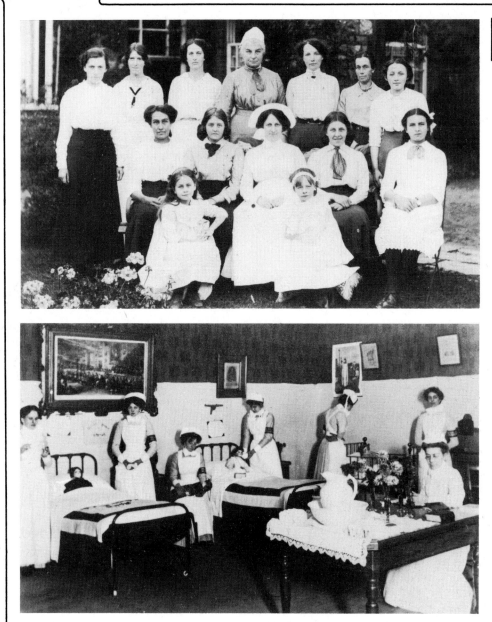

Well there we have Auntie Mabel in full nursing gig, and a lot of these others are composed of her nursing friends. They don't mean anything to me. I don't know in what kind of order, or in how many places, or even when she was trained. But there was a postcard around addressed from Mother to her which may have been sent when she was in training. I saw it was sent to Firvale Hospital, and I think another address was Bagley in Cheshire.[1]

1. Mabel's poetry notebook contains entries from Sheffield Union Hospital, 1909–11; Firvale Hospital, Sheffield, 1912; Bagley Sanatorium, Cheshire, 1913; and Lees Nursing Home, Oldham, September, 1914. [M. W.]

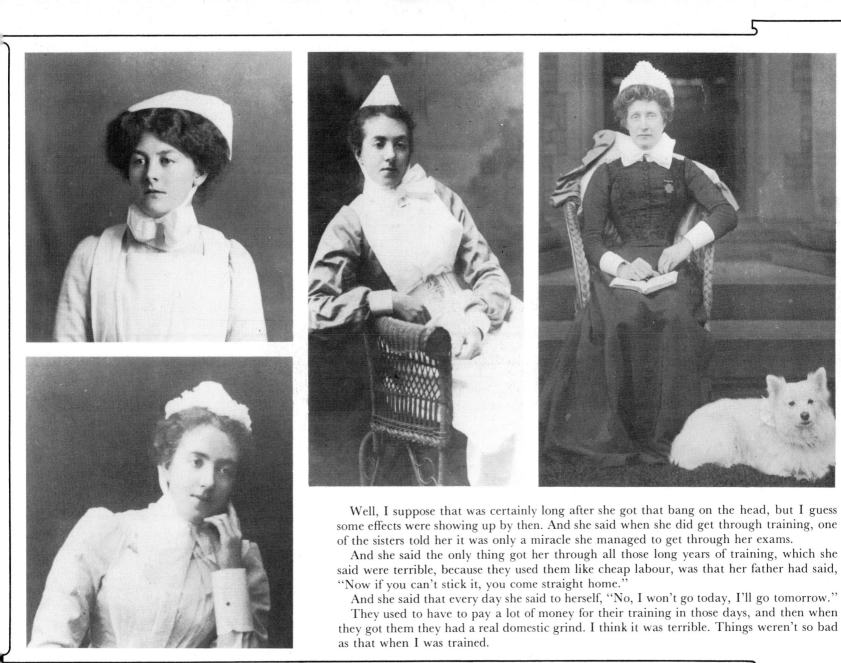

Well, I suppose that was certainly long after she got that bang on the head, but I guess some effects were showing up by then. And she said when she did get through training, one of the sisters told her it was only a miracle she managed to get through her exams.

And she said the only thing got her through all those long years of training, which she said were terrible, because they used them like cheap labour, was that her father had said, "Now if you can't stick it, you come straight home."

And she said that every day she said to herself, "No, I won't go today, I'll go tomorrow."

They used to have to pay a lot of money for their training in those days, and then when they got them they had a real domestic grind. I think it was terrible. Things weren't so bad as that when I was trained.

Funny how nurses tend to remember people's illnesses without remembering their names.

SCARLET FEVER
JULY, 1914

FIBROIDS
1912

OVARIAN CYST
OCTOBER, 1914

It probably would have been easier for her, though, if she hadn't been hit on the head. How it happened was that my grandfather was a great cricket fan. His great joy was to take the whole family on a cricket fortnight at Scarborough, putting up at Truefitt's boarding house. It was quite routine for him to do this each year. Well on one of these occasions Mother and Auntie Mabel were out riding and Mabel's horse, not Charlie, the family horse, but a hired one, threw her and she landed on her head. I think Mother said she was unconscious for days, even weeks. And all her early promise as a musician and so on, went off. Mother said as a child growing up at school Mabel had come home with all these prizes and what not, and was called the clever one. And suddenly it all seemed to fizzle out. Mother said they put it down to these weeks of hospital in Scarborough. She must have had some brain damage I imagine.

Then afterwards she must have had a terrible experience during the First World War. And this morbid streak seemed to arrive from somewhere. No one else in the family seemed to have it. The circumstances of her life must have brought it on. She had all these awful depressing pictures around of nuns sitting by open graves, and half dead soldiers hanging by their legs, and all that. Yet she was very soft hearted, and if anyone came to her with a sob-story, they could have walked away with the world.

That's my mum next to Mrs. Truefitt. I don't know any of the others.

IN THE SUMMER OF WHICH THE PEACE OF EUROPE IS DISRUPTED BY THE OUTBREAK OF A
DREADFUL WAR . . .

THE WAR BEGINS!

THE WESTERN FRONT

The actual causes of the First World War are still a matter of debate to some extent, but Auntie Mabel doubtless shared the views of most Britons at the time. The violation of Belgian neutrality by Germany was enough to make war a moral imperative for most, and there was no shortage of volunteers, either soldiers or nurses.

Although there was much movement over the countryside in 1914, when the German army got to within forty miles of Paris, and again in the months preceding the armistice, the middle years of the war were, on the Western Front, very static. The opposing armies were entrenched along a battle line running virtually from the sea to the Swiss frontier, and devastating battles were fought for minimal territorial advantage. The Allies always hoped the German line would give; but it never did, and it was not until the collapse of the Eastern Front in 1918 and the arrival of American reinforcements that anything decisive happened.

The thick line on the map shows the battle line late in 1917, but may be taken as generally representative of a long period of war. Alsace and Lorraine had been in German hands since the Franco-Prussian war; the other areas of France and Belgium east of the line, and of course Luxembourg, were occupied by Germany. Holland and Switzerland were neutral.

ALSACE IN 1870
MIGHT AND COURAGE

ALSACE IN 1870
THERE! THEY SHOT OUR MOTHER

ALSACE AND LORRAINE
TORN FROM FRANCE 1871

I AM FRANCE. YOU ARE ALSACE,
I BRING YOU THE KISS OF FRANCE.
JOFFRE.

General Joffre was a veteran soldier who became French commander-in-chief during the earlier part of the war. He was dismissed in December, 1916.

23

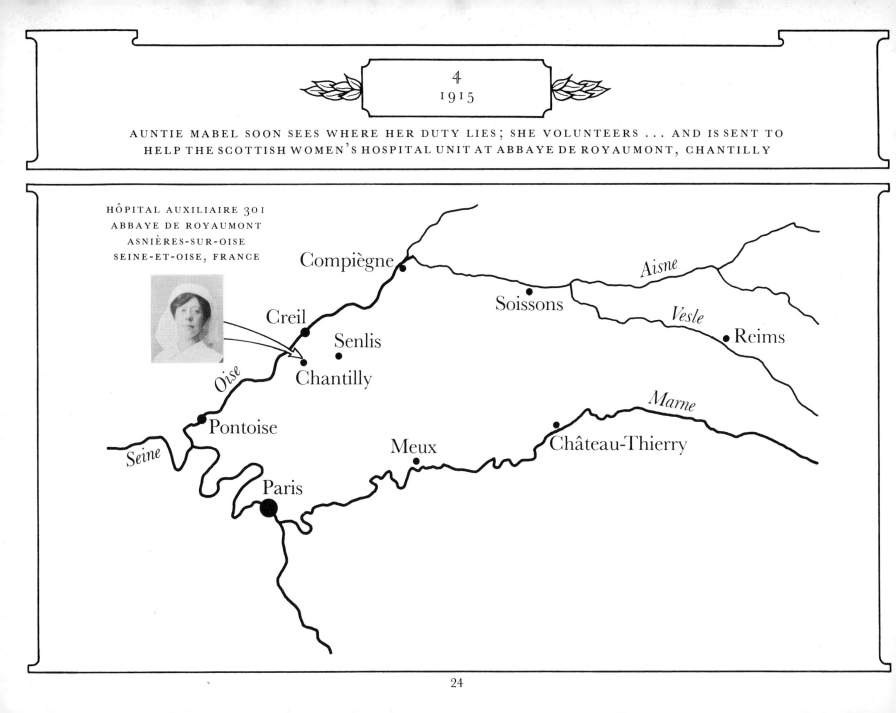

4
1915

AUNTIE MABEL SOON SEES WHERE HER DUTY LIES; SHE VOLUNTEERS ... AND IS SENT TO
HELP THE SCOTTISH WOMEN'S HOSPITAL UNIT AT ABBAYE DE ROYAUMONT, CHANTILLY

HÔPITAL AUXILIAIRE 301
ABBAYE DE ROYAUMONT
ASNIÈRES-SUR-OISE
SEINE-ET-OISE, FRANCE

Compiègne

Aisne

Soissons

Vesle

Creil

Senlis

Reims

Oise

Chantilly

Marne

Pontoise

Meux

Château-Thierry

Seine

Paris

A FRENCH HOSPITAL UNDER THE DIRECTION OF SUFFRAGETTES[1]

A Model of Organisation

When, last December, Miss Hamilton and some of her companions, who come like herself from Scotland, took possession of Royaumont Abbey in order to transform it into an auxiliary hospital, they found little more than the bare walls of large cold rooms with vast vaulted ceilings. These buildings, which date from the thirteenth century, are in a perfect state of preservation, but as uncomfortable as they could possibly be, as especially befits a monastery bereft of its oblates.

Nothing was installed in this property, which had passed into the possession of MM. GOUIN, whose name recalls a gory drama in which the rôle of the miserable victim fell, during the course of a railway journey, to the venerable grandmother of the family.

There was, in this edifice, neither a kitchen, nor heating of any kind, and it was to be wondered how the last inhabitants of this lodging had lived, stranded in the Middle Ages with respect to comfort.

Certainly, in this cheerful part of the Oise Valley, which is bordered by the forest of Carnelle, quite close to the little town of Viarmes, the frame which surrounds the old abbey, hidden in the woodland of a park with a royal aspect, is worthy of the building. The majestic galleries of the cloister surround a courtyard, whose flower-studded verdure catches the vaporised droplets of a softly murmuring fountain. Here and there the moss has speckled the arcades of the monastery with felted green cloth. Far away, the curve of the river seems to encompass the countryside with a moving belt of flashing silver ribbon.

But ladies and young women from Britain, notwithstanding their love of Nature's poetry, told themselves that they had come to France to bring their ministrations to the wounded, and not just to admire grave gothic architecture set in lovely countryside.

They therefore set to work, practically and energetically, and one month later Auxiliary Hospital 301 began to function. Without despoiling the old vaulting, which evokes the memory of the monastic life of another age, completely modern equipment was set up in the empty building, and from the stained glass windows the saints, with leaded outlines, seemed, thenceforth, to smile down on the heroic French wounded who are tended, with tireless devotion, by the valiant Scottish women.

Because this hospital has a singular feature: its staff is exclusively female, and is affiliated to the "National Union of Women's Suffrage Societies".

These ladies are, therefore, suffragettes. They do not belong, it behoves us to say, to the revolutionary, or better, rowdy, element of that federation. These ladies assert their rights peacefully. But, well aware of these rights, they wished above all to do their duty, and they vied with each other, these well-born women, to lay claim to a job amongst our wounded, even to the humble or toilsome functions of ward-assistants or kitchen-maids.

Mrs. Harley, the sister of General French,[2] has been until just recently the "mother superior" of the abbey. She has now gone on to Troyes, where she is equipping another hospital, and has been replaced by Miss Loudon, who received us with the most perfect grace, and enabled us to visit, in the company of Miss Hamilton, the general secretary, the various sections of the Seine-et-Oise branch of the Scottish Women's Hospitals.

The medical and surgical services are under the direction of Miss Ivens, the chief doctor, who is assisted by Misses Nicholson, Hancock, Rutherford and Proctor, and by Mrs. Berry, these all doctors or surgeons. Mrs. Savill, a doctor also, has charge of radiography, and Mrs. (Professor) Butler heads the bacteriological laboratory.

The equipping and maintenance of the hospital devolves upon the feminist society, the head office of which is in Edinburgh, Scotland. Two other sister hospitals have been established in Serbia.

At Royaumont Abbey two hundred beds are available for wounded Frenchmen. These two hundred beds are disposed in six wards, admirably maintained in every respect, and the soldiers, with whom we were able to speak freely and privately, never failed to tell the praises of the staff who lavish attention on them.

We have been present at operations, and at dressings, and wish everyone could see the minute precautions and the delicacy with which the feminine hands of the doctors, and the qualified nurses who assist them, tend to the often frightful wounds of our brave combatants.

The staff of this hospital is entirely female, as we have said. No exception is made to this rule.[3] The cars and mobile ambulances are regularly driven by "mécaniciennes", who could with advantage be emulated by many Parisian drivers.

As we were about to take our leave of her, Miss Loudon, the director of this model establishment, said to us, in a typically feminine remark: "We are lacking something for our patients, which unfortunately the French hospital rules forbid us to bring into the wards, namely flowers, which make life so much more cheerful for the wounded who are confined to bed."

A little soldier – a law student – who was undergoing treatment and who had overheard answered prettily and simply – "Madame, in the hearts of all of you here, compassion and devotion flourish. And those are, for us, the most beautiful flowers in the world, because they remind us of the tenderness of our mothers, and our sisters."

I am not sure that, at that moment, tears were not to be seen in the eyes of Miss Loudon, who hid her emotion by giving me a vigorous "shake hands", accompanied by a friendly "good-bye".

---

1. See also Appendix B.

2. General Sir John French, commander-in-chief, B.E.F., 1914–15.

3. This no longer seemed to be the case during Mabel's time at the hospital.

ROYAUMONT HOSPITAL – A GROUP OF
WOUNDED AND NURSES

Hôpital de ROYAUMONT. — Groupe de Blessés et Infirmières.

On Active Service[1]

c/o S.W.H.[2]
Hôpital Auxiliaire 301
Abbaye de Royaumont
Asnières-sur-Oise
Seine-et-Oise, France

30.3.15

ROYAUMONT ABBEY

13. ABBAYE DE ROYAUMONT

This is one view of the Abbey. It has been empty about 10 years, since the nuns left it. It is a very large place with beautiful grounds. We are 30 miles from the fighting lines with the trenches quite close here.

Have not heard the guns yet, but they are often very loud.

We missed the 11.20 train from Paris – that nurse's fault – and had to wait till 5.30.

The ambulance "Hallowe'en" met us at Viarmes station. I need not stamp letters – *and you need not if you put* "*Active Service*". One Doctor has been between the lines bringing out the wounded.

They say there will be a big battle this week and we shall get the men straight from the trenches. I was very sick crossing. Hope you will enjoy Wales.

Love from Mab.

1. The postcards which are reproduced, with or without their texts, are from Mabel Jeffery to her family in England, unless otherwise stated. Captions of cards are given in translation from languages other than English only when their material is not self-evident, or when the caption is of particular importance. When communications to Mabel are given, (F) at the beginning indicates that the original is in French. [M. W., J. C.]
2. Scottish Women's Hospitals.

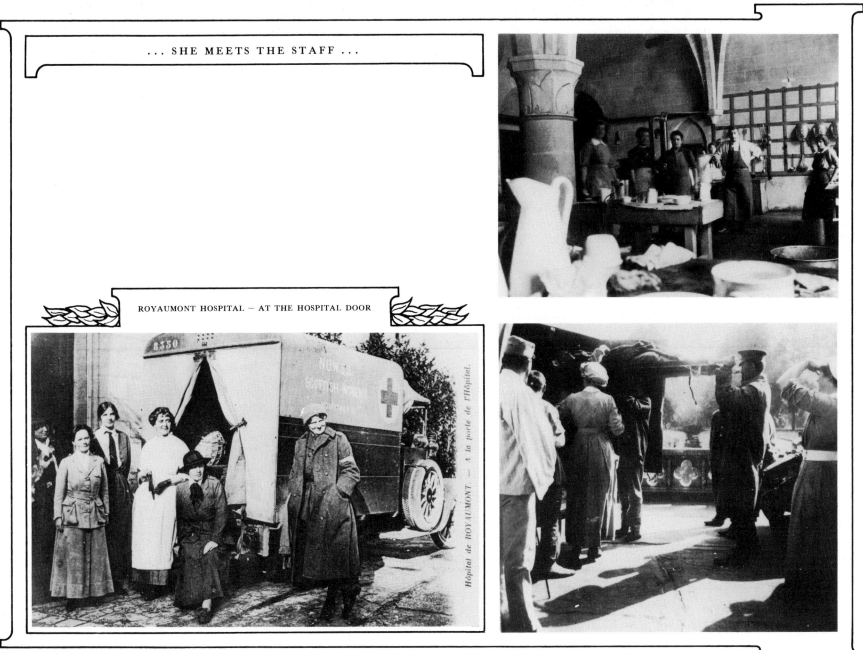

... SHE MEETS THE STAFF ...

ROYAUMONT HOSPITAL — AT THE HOSPITAL DOOR

Hôpital de ROYAUMONT — A la porte de l'Hôpital.

"One n' all"   "Hallowe'en"[2]

Mr. Inglis   Mr. Oldham   Miss McGregor   Miss Williams

1. The word "*ambulance*" was used both to describe an individual vehicle to transport sick and wounded, of the sort shown here, and a mobile army unit which could be attached to an established hospital (pp. 69, 72), or transferred from there to the fighting front (pp. 79, 82, 84).

2. "Hallowe'en" had met Auntie Mabel on arrival at the nearby town of Viarmes; see p. 28.

Active Service, Croix-Rouge française. Royaumont, 6.4.15

Am sorry I did not see Father's envelope until I had addressed one – but it will come in my next letter. Hope you received all safely? Are you feeling better now Mother? I hope you had a nice Easter. It has been very wet here the last few days. You will see by the cards this is a fine place. One I had just addressed to Harry I think is where we have our meals now. At first we dined in the cellar. We go to Paris about once a month to get a bath, I think she charges us F 2.50^c.

Some of the patients have been wounded 3 or 4 times. One new man has been in the trenches since August – right through the war. Let me know how the war goes on.

With much love from Mabel.

P.S. They are afraid this hospital may be closed down, as the people at the Château are sorry now they lent it.[1] The monks here used to dig their graves every day.

1. The Abbey was located in the grounds of the Gouins' château (pp. 26, 46).

ROYAUMONT ABBEY

21. ABBAYE DE ROYAUMONT

Frémont, Édit., Beaumont-sur-Oise

Frémont, édit.

9. Abbaye de ROYAUMONT

Sat. night. 17.4.15

Many thanks for Father's letter received today. This is near the wards "Queen Mary" and "Blanche of Castille" and is where St. Louis of France had the leper room, – perhaps the fountain outside is where they used to drink – about 1230.

It has been colder today but yesterday the sun was very hot. There have been a lot of flowers in the grounds – violets, cowslips etc. I have sent a card to Aunt Fanny. I do not know Uncle Jim's address.

Thank you for sending to the Scottish Women's Hospital. Was it especially for the Abbaye de Royaumont hospital? You must take any of my money for anything you want. I dreamt Father had murdered us all – it is the food that makes me dream.

We have 3 of these Red Cross chauffeurs here – men – also several women, they take the ambulances to Creil every day for patients. I think there are 4 ambulances altogether. Many thanks for papers.

Much love from Mab.

P.S. We should like some more cigs. and a packet of tea.

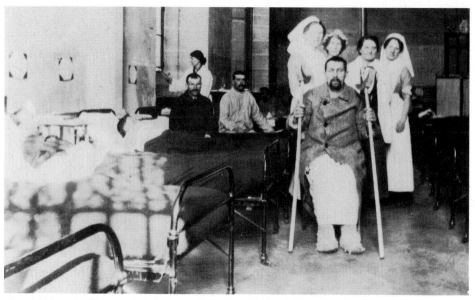

(Above) Marguerite d'Ecosse Ward   (Below) Blanche de Castille Ward

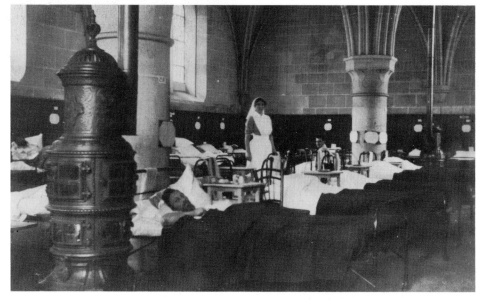

1. Some rules for self-conduct from Mabel's notebooks, dated Abbaye de Royaumont, 1915, read:

"Finish every day and be done with it. You have done what you could. Some blunders and absurdities no doubt crept in; forget them as soon as you can. Tomorrow is a new day, begin it well and serenely, and with too high a spirit to be cumbered with your old nonsense. The day is all that is good and fair. It is too dear with its hopes and aspirations to waste a moment upon the yesterday."

(Above) Jeanne d'Arc Ward   (Below) Millicent Ward

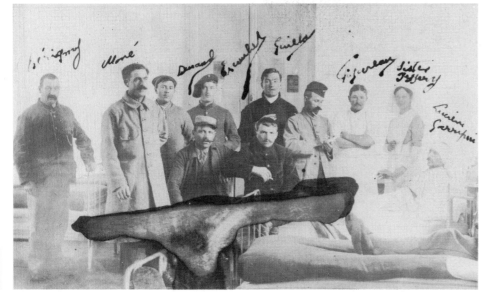

1014.   La chère maison.
          Home! home! sweet, sweet home!

(FIDES)

1.5.15

This is something like our patients. They come in with their guns, etc. – which of course are all labelled with their names. One man has the "Service Militaire" (am not sure of the name but the highest Fr. medal. So=to our V.C.) Am quite well today. In "Millicent" ward we have bullet schrapnel and bomb wounds, etc. In "Jeanne d'Arc" men crippled with rheumatism, etc.

41. SENLIS - Guerre Septembre 1914 - A cet endroit fut fusillé
et enterré provisoirement M. ODENT, maire de Senlis
SENLIS - War September 1914 - In this place shooted and buried
M. ODENT, Senlis mayors   A.B.

SENLIS AFTER THE GERMANS HAD PASSED THROUGH

SENLIS après le passage des Allemands (Septembre 1914).
Rue Bellon, Carrefour de la Licorne.

Saturday, May 29th, 1915

Dearest Mother and Father,
Have just had the undergarments, Mother dear. Thank you *very* much, they look very nice and cool. Yes thank you, the tea is *very* nice. Do you think you have all my letters now?

Yesterday a V.A.D. "*chauffeuse*"[1] took 5 of the sisters (including me) to Senlis – the Germans were there about September. Many houses are in ruins; I have got p.cs. to send you. We left at 1.30 and got back at 4.30, and had a little tea there in a café.

We have an Egyptian in with half a finger blown off – it was bad when he came in. He says he has been fighting side by side with the English soldiers, as far as I could make out. Dr. asked him how he was tonight and he said (as they always do) "Just as you like" – or "Just as God likes". A lot are leaving. The other sister is going on to La Panne.

It would be lovely if you met me in London but it is rather soon yet to think about that isn't it, with the war no further on?

1. Voluntary Aid Detachment member. See Appendix A.

10.6.15

Do you like the hot weather? Am writing again tomorrow.
    Love to all, M.

34

Friday, June 11th, 1915

Am wearing a ring made out of a piece of shell – German – the patients make a great many of them – they nearly all have them. After the enemy have been firing they get those pieces of albuminium (*sic*) and make rings, etc. out of it and we call them the "*bôches*" (*sic*).

The ambulances have already been twice today and will come in again tonight. It is the first time we have had any in before 8 pm at night; they have asked us to have plenty of beds ready. Please tell me if the poetry arrives safely in this.[1] I have a translation of it to send. The poet wrote out several copies for us.

With love Mab.

1. See following pages.

SENLIS après le passage des Allemands (Septembre 1914).
La Sous-Préfecture.

THE SUB-PREFECTURE.
SENLIS AFTER THE GERMANS HAD PASSED THROUGH

THE GREAT WAR 1914–15. JUNCTION OF TWO
FIRST-LINE TRENCHES IN THE ARRAS REGION

Saturday, June 12th, 1915

Thanks for yours today. So glad you liked the handky, and so sorry I did not get one for Father, but got two more for Maud and Arnold. (Have not sent them yet.) What do you think, I cut the cake you sent last night and found your letter inside, was so pleased and have written to Grandma today. Louie Wyld says Willie has to work on a farm from 6–6, with an hour off for dinner.

This is where a lot of fighting is going on, the men in last night said they left the trenches and charged with bayonets and the German guns simply swept them down – they all say the slaughter on both sides is terrible. The Egyptian with half a thumb off is almost ready for going, the "eye" man has gone – but I should not have thought again to the war.

Aux Fées de Royaumont.

Nymphes de Royaumont! qui de vos doigts divins
Avez bâti ce nid au milieu des sapins
Je ne veux point quitter ce joli coin de France
Où les Anges et les fleurs guérissent la souffrance
Sans dire à Vous Merci. Aux maîtres de ces lieux
Qui érigea la vertu et la foi d'un Roi pieux
S'intéressant encore des splendeurs d'un autre âge
J'adresse tout d'abord un respectueux hommage.
Au Roi Georges, à son peuple, à la Reine Mary
Que déjà dans son cœur tout Français a béni
Je souhaite que bientôt le char de la Victoire
En couronnant la nôtre les conduise à la gloire
Que la Force et l'Amour des trois peuples unis
Triomphant des vautours venus de Germanie
Dans une ère de paix préparent pour toujours
Aux batailles passées l'impossible retour.
Quant à vous chères Miss dont les soins empressés
Entourent nuit et jour nos chers petits blessés
D'indissolubles liens, vous enveloppez l'intensité
Et semez dans nos cœurs la foi la plus ardente;
Sur notre sol meurtri, vos lauriers plus nombreux
Recueilliront de jour en jour des lauriers nombreux
Et côté de nos frères, ils luttent vaillamment
Et pour la même cause succombent noblement
Tandis que vous leurs sœurs, offrandant nos souffrances
Disputez à la mort les enfants de la France

D'acier le même trempé des armes meurtrières
Se transforme en vos mains en lames humanitaires
Et vos doigts délicats douce Miss Nicholson
Sans le corps palpitant s'enfoncent sans frisson
Tandis que dans un rêve Miss Irene, Miss Steinworth
Sur la table légère, votre patient s'endort
Sous le charme confiant que votre science inspire
Et le voir au réveil rechercher ce sourire
Baume réconfortant au sur les plaies saignantes
Vous répandez sans trêve femmes compatissantes.
Je n'oublierai jamais le dévouement constant
Tous ces soins maternels et ce zèle touchant
Que l'intègre Maxwell, la bonne Jefferies
Prodiguent à toute heure aux pauvres corps meurtris.
J'emporterai en m'en allant un souvenir précieux
De la franche gaité, de vos charmes gracieux
Suave Miss Harley, aimable Miss Allan;
L'éclat de votre rire, coquette miss Chapman
À l'oreille charmée résonnera encore
À côté de celui de la belle Miss Moore.
Si ma modeste lyre, je voudrais pour chacune
Faire vibrer l'archet; que du bois blond ou brun
Son sein renferme un cœur plus précieux que l'or.
Au printemps de la vie du choix la douleur
Puisse je vous bientôt par des jours de bonheur
Forcée chaque minute à nos chères pensée
Et ton rêve secret par mes vœux exaucé.

Et toi gai rossignol qui charmes mes nuits blanches
Pourquoi l'oiseau du soir sous les branches?
Dis moi petit oiseau la crainte qui t'oppresse
Lorsque de l'amitié, je t'offre la caresse
J'aurais voulu pourtant avant de te quitter
Par un baiser bien doux, envers toi m'acquitter
Mais le temps presse et là haut le canon tonne
J'entends sa voix, de la même l'écho résonne
Je vais reprendre au feu la place de celui
Dont le cœur s'est éteint, dont l'âme s'est enfui
Adieu donc! je te quitte asile séculaire
De charitables Fées auguste sanctuaire;
De ma reconnaissance qu'un dernier vœu t'inspire
Avant que de mon luth, l'ultime note expire;
Puisse le malheureux faux meurtri
Trouver sur son chemin toujours un Royaumont.

Adieu en témoignage de reconnaissance

The translation to which Mabel refers in the cards dated June 11th and
June 18th, 1915, on pp. 35 and 39, is unfortunately lost. Feeling that a
prose translation would convey nothing of the flavour of this poem we
give it here in a verse translation, such as, we feel, Mabel herself might
have contrived.

TO THE SPRITES OF ROYAUMONT

O Royaumont nymphs, who with fingers divine
Have constructed this nest midst a forest of pine,
I cannot go forth from this fair French domain,
Where angels and flowers relieve us from pain,
Without saying thanks! You, in charge of this place,
Who exalt here a pious king's[1] virtue and grace,
And make once again the old splendours shine out,
To you I address first my homage devout.
For King George, and his people, and Mary the Queen,
Who blessed in all Frenchmen's hearts ever have been,
I wish that the chariot of victory soon may
Lead them, and lead us, to the glorious day.
May the strength and the love of three peoples unite
In defeating the vultures of Germany's spite,
And prepare, in an era of peace for all men,
Against battles which never must happen again.
As for you, my dear Misses whose soft eager care
Enfolds day and night our sick comrades' despair,
You sow faith in our hearts, and with permanent bands
Make firm the *entente* that unites our two lands.
On our ravaged homeland your soldiers so brave
Gather daily more laurels, defying the grave;
Alongside our brothers they gallantly fight
And nobly they fall in the same cause of right;
Whilst you, their dear sisters, our sufferings ease
And from death's hungry jaws France's children you seize.
The tempered steel whereof grim weapons are made,
In your hands is changed into humanity's blade.
Your fingers, Miss Nicholson, dip without qualm
Into soft throbbing bodies that lie still and calm.
You, Miss Ivens, Miss Heyworth, inspire by your science
A confident spell; win your patient's compliance:
He sleeps through his treatment; I see him on waking
Look round for your smiles, as the spell's gently breaking,
Strengthening balm which on war's grievous sore,
Compassionate women, you ceaselessly pour.

I'll never forget the unswerving devotion,
The motherly tenderness, touching emotion,
That honest Miss Maxwell, Miss Jeffery so good,
Bring to bodies all covered with bruises and blood.
I will carry a precious remembrance away
Of the gracious behaviour, and frankness, of gay
And tender Miss Harley, Miss Alan so kind;
And the sound of Miss Chapman's sweet laugh, left behind,
Will echo again in charmed memory's store
Along with the laughter of lovely Miss Moore.
The strings of my modest lyre gladly I'll set
To vibrate for each one, whether blonde or brunette;
Whether daughter of poor folk, or great lord's own dear,
In your breasts, hearts more precious than gold you all bear.
In life's springtime you choose to keep company with dread;
May you soon see each minute spent by our bedhead
Rewarded with days in which happiness teems,
And may God grant fulfilment to your secret dreams.
Ah nightingale, charm of my sleepless nights, who
The other night into the green branches flew
O say, little bird, what dark fears may oppress
When in friendship I offer to you a caress?
I would but have wished before leaving you here
To discharge all my debts with a sweet kiss, my dear.
But time waits for no man! I hear the guns pound,
And out of the battle the echoes resound.
I return to the fire in the place of one dead,
Whose heart is extinguished, whose spirit is fled.
So, Farewell then, I leave you now, sanctuary, and
Abode of good fairies, majestic and grand;
And out of my debt to you one last wish bear,
Before my lute's final note fades in the air:
May the downcast and dying, the sick and distressed
Find always a Royaumont offering rest.

Offered in recognition of my debt to you.

1. St. Louis, who was Louis IX of France (reigned 1226–70).

The pictures she sends home are usually depressing, but if her intention is to educate the family in the pity of war she doesn't often carry it over to the reverse. The card below is one of many propaganda cards reproducing paintings (for others see pp. 54, 99).

E. J. DELAHAYE – "THE FIRST VICTIM".
ABBÉ HENNEQUIN SHOT DOWN BY THE BARBARIANS
AT MOYENVIC

Sunday, June 13th, 1915

Thanks for letter today – dated 9th. Will send you as many p.cs. as possible as you like to have them and I have so many for you. You need not stamp your letters but please address "Miss".

Thanks for all the news. You did fine – re the eggs at B'stone.[1] Have not yet received word of the coat; don't send anything else, dear. I will do what I can with the packing when the time comes. Wasn't it strange I "trained" as a nurse and now I feel quite satisfied.

We often use the French words amongst the English – "*cheval*" means "horse", it is not very nice but makes good gravy! We are very busy. The Egyptian goes out today. They all say they get mown down like hay. We have often visitors.

Love from Mab.

1. This is Bolsterstone, a small village near Deepcar.

Friday, June 18th, 1915

Thank you very much for the pen – it will be very useful indeed if I can find any ink. Also many thanks for newspapers. Do you think conscription will come in? Glad you think all is well but the end is not in view yet?

Our worst case has been all through the war – his father is wounded – his wife and children are prisoners. Our nicest patient – a sergeant – has three brothers fighting also his father who is wounded. In the ambulance train last night at Creil were two German prisoners – both with one arm gone – guarded by three French soldiers with bayonets. Thanks for all news. The enclosed p.c. is from the sergeant who wrote the poetry; did you get it and the translation.

THE WAR OF 1914–15. IN THE FOREST OF COMPIÈGNE PARIS BUSES ARE USED FOR PROVISIONING.

ROYAUMONT ABBEY

11. ABBAYE DE ROYAUMONT

28.6.15.

This is now our dining hall. We have no breakable china or crockery at all – tin things. There are three tables near the "pulpit" – the Doctors', the V.A.D.s' and the Sisters'.

Did you know you had not fastened up the last p.c. again – although it was stamped? Would you like to send a few cigs – for the "*soldats dans la salle Millicent, par M.J.*" They are very keen on cigs-*Anglaise*.

Much love, Mab.

THE BANKS OF THE OISE — AT BORAN

£01. LES BORDS DE L'OISE — BORAN

le 3 July, 1915

Dearest Mother,
Many thanks for your letter today – also the p.c. today. Did I not thank you for the little calendar? Have not had much time lately for writing but have sent several p.cs.

Have not yet got Father's note books but *today* had a paper to sign for a parcel at the station so perhaps that is it. I do not think the French soldiers would like texts, and we are not allowed to give them – for the most part they have no religion. But little calendars, etc. they like very much. Anything for a souvenir.

This bridge was blown up, with the others on the river, by the French: to prevent the Germans crossing when they were making their way to Paris. I went with another sister last Wednesday: we crossed the river of course in a ferry boat. Today is very hot. Many have been off with mosquito bites – my arms are a sight – swollen and scarred but am much better now, – it does not make me ill at all as it does some of the others.

Many thanks for papers.

(This text is on two postcards. The second only is reproduced.)

5.7.15

Many thanks for parcels received today, they will come in most useful for souvenirs. The "eatables" were only crumbs but thanks all the same.

W.B.L. Y.E.M.

La Guerre 1914-1915. — Région de SOISSONS. Canon de 155 long.

Visa 2 Paris
J. Courcier, 8, Rue Simon-le-Franc, Paris

A VIEW FROM HOME

A VIEW AT THE FRONT

NEW MILL BRIDGE

Broomfield,
Deepcar Near Sheffield from Lucy Jeffery
10.7.15

Dearest Mabel,
Your father received the *handkerchief* and card and was very pleased. I also wrote you last Saturday, and posted you box of books small ones, with letter enclosed, hope you get them safely. I stamp and leave envelopes unfastened thinking you might get them a little sooner. Are you keeping quite well dear, so glad you liked the books your Father sent. Have you got the cake Mrs. May sent – you write when you can dearest
    love from Mother

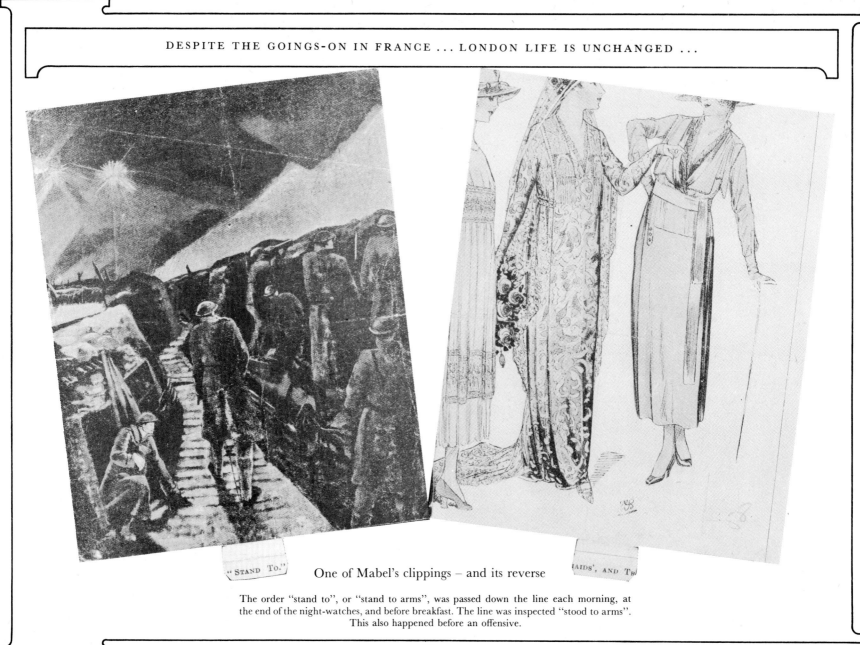

"STAND TO."

AIDS', AND TH

One of Mabel's clippings – and its reverse

The order "stand to", or "stand to arms", was passed down the line each morning, at
the end of the night-watches, and before breakfast. The line was inspected "stood to arms".
This also happened before an offensive.

July 19th, 1915

Thanks for yours. I could take a holiday in about another two months but I think I would rather do without it as it is "for the war"; if I came home I might not be able to begin work again. The little French books are much appreciated.

Very sorry to hear about Mr. Sampson. Saw Canon Wilson's will in the last paper from home. Perhaps I can send you the address of some soldier so that you could send a few cigarettes direct to the trenches. For several nights now we have had *very* few *blessés* in. We have all of us got a "*bôche*" ring and I have two; the men make them out of the German shells.

Love to all. Mab.

This is, of course, the picture of a widow, – they say most women in Paris wear black now.

REGIONAL FRENCH MOURNING COSTUME

Deux-Sèvres - 43 - PARTHENAY - Costume de Deuil
E. Cordier O, édit., Parthenay. Reproduction interdite

LOOK, IT'S CALLING US, THE SEA,
TO DARDANELLES AND VICTORY[1]

FORWARD, CHILDREN!!

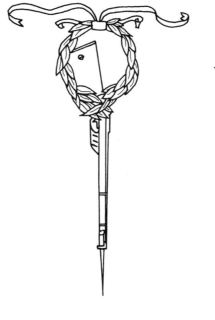

1. The Allies in fact failed miserably in the Dardanelles, at least in so far as their primary objectives were concerned. The French in any case had no enthusiasm for any operation which would draw troops from the Western Front.

Louis Walser,
30th Infantry,
32nd Company,
St. Pierre d'Alligny,
Savoie

(F)

August 2nd, 1915

Dear Sister,
I thank you very much for your friendly card, equally for your kind wishes.
I am completely cured and ready to go back to the war.
Yours with respect and friendship
L. Walser

EN GUERRE . DECHARGEMENT D'UNE PIÈCE
THE WAR DISCHARGING OF A GUN .

La Guerre 1914-1915   GLANNES — Ce qui reste du village après le passage des barbares.
209 R.P. Paris   (Meuse)   Remains of the village after the barbarians's passage.

... SHE IS FIGHTING HER OWN WAR ... AGAINST
THE FLEA !

August 5th, 1915

Many thanks for letter this A.M. I was thinking of asking Mother to send me two more flea pads. Could they come one at a time in an envelope. I think the others lost their smell with always being wet. The perspiration is running down our faces all the time, but today is just a little cooler. A flea kept me awake last night. I put the other pads in my night dress sleeves and then let it go to the wash. The Dr. comes round any time after 7 a.m. and we try to get the treatment done before that, then I cannot get to my room through the day as the night people sleep there, and six sisters left yesterday so there are very few left now, and we are on the *salles* almost all day. All the sisters are going soon. I hope you will like Blackpool. Had a card from Gladys from there.
    Love from Mab.

THE ABBOT'S PALACE

ABBAYE DE ROYAUMONT — ASNIÉRES-SUR-OISE (S.-&-O.)

Frémont édit., Beaumont-sur-Oise

Le Palais Abbatial

Abbaye de Royaumont, August 7th, 1915

The patients are sleeping out now, in the cloisters at the back of the Abbey. The grounds all round are very large and beautiful. Shall soon have been here six months, but do not know yet if I am coming home, or may go on to Belgium. Hope you and Mr. Hatton are both much stronger now. How is Gertie. Last night we had seven wounded in. They sent word from Creil that we might be having a lot in at any time of the day or night. Have you been to Blackpool lately. Don't go and work too hard again!

I do not smoke much, Mother, only a little to soothe my nerves.

August 11th, 1915

Have I sent you many views of the Abbey? This is in the castle, where the Guinens[1] live, who have lent the Abbey for a hospital. The grounds are beautiful but of course the war overshadows everything. We are not getting so many patients in just now, they say the fighting is more in other places. The ambulances go every night to fetch the wounded. You would be sorry to hear about Mr. Sampson.

Love to all, from Mabel.

1. Actually Gouins.

Sunday night. 22.8.15

Thank you for your letter, Mother, and Father's today. The weather is cooler now so am wearing my thicker stockings. Have just jumped out of bed to look at some sort of aircraft. Sister said it was like a big star – it made more noise than usual, but was passed before I saw it.

Yesterday in my ward had seven *blessés* – two have very bad hands – their fingers were lopped off on the field. They are all very tired and have slept nearly all day.

The cars are to be at Creil at 5 a.m. tomorrow. Some French general has been round today, so we have been busy. The two sisters who came out with me from London are in the same ward now, one on days and one on nights but I am in charge. Hope you will enjoy Llandudno. Have finished the Quinphos[1] and feel better for it. Am so thankful to say I think I can last out till the end of the war, but after that I might sleep for ever. – Hope you are in bed now.

W.B.L. Mab.

1. A suspension of quinine in phosphate of iron, taken as a tonic.

271. Guerre de 1914-15 — St.-OMER - Troupes Anglaise sur la Grand'place
L'H. Paris

ST.-OMER – ENGLISH TROOPS IN THE SQUARE

Royaumont, *le 27 Août*, 1915 *(card not shown)*

Thank you for yours today, dear Mother, from Llandudno. This is the second I have addressed there, but in the future will send home. I got the first lot of stockings (one white pair). Shall begin to wear them as it has turned very hot again. We have been very busy with new *blessés*, the cars have been going at all hours.

The theatre sister today heard that her brother was killed at the Dardanelles. One of the "Paris" cases has improved very much – the other one may have to have his leg amputated.

Tomorrow some generals (French and English) are coming, and one day, "Papa Joffre".

Hope you are having nice weather and all enjoying the holiday. Thanks for the *Queen*, there is a nice piece in about Senlis – shall keep it to send to you to keep for me.

W.B.L. Mab.

Military Romance
A KISS COSTS NOTHING, AND MAKES COSY
PRESENT DAYS, THE FUTURE ROSY

(F) France, Royaumont

17.9.15

In affectionate remembrance and friendship from one of your patients. When will you return?
Marcel Renard
Salle Millicent

Sister M. E. Jeffery
Broomfield
Déepcar (*sic*)
Nr. Sheffied (*sic*)
Angleterre

October 26th, 1915, 11.45 p.m.

Dearest Mother,
Many thanks for the pretty card I got this morning. Please keep the *Queen* as long as you like, I generally take about a week to read one.

Sister O'Rorke was very much upset about Miss Cavell's[1] death, she was the Matron of the Home in connection with the hospital in Brussels where she and her friend were. She said she had always thought of her as another Florence Nightingale, as she always seemed to be working, and although she was about 50 years old, never seemed to have more than three or four hours sleep.

I ate some of the chocolate you gave me for my birthday this morning when I was out, it was very nice indeed.

This is where we go "boating" sometimes.

With much love, from Mabel.

1. Edith Cavell (1865–1915) was a nurse shot by the Germans in Brussels on October 12th, 1915. Organiser and manager of the St. Gilles hospital in Brussels and first matron of the Birkendael medical institute there, she was accused of concealing French and English soldiers and helping them escape, as well as assisting Belgians of military age to go to the front.

CHÂTEAU DE ROYAUMONT, NEAR VIARMES – THE LAKE

Château de Royaumont, près Viarmes - La Pièce d'eau

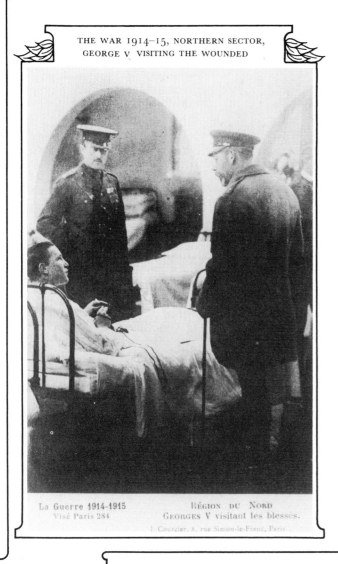

THE WAR 1914–15, NORTHERN SECTOR,
GEORGE V VISITING THE WOUNDED

La Guerre 1914-1915
Visé Paris 284

RÉGION DU NORD
GEORGES V visitant les blessés.

1. Courcier, 8, rue Simon-le-Franc, Paris

October 26th, 1915, 11.30 p.m.

My dear Father,
Thank you very much for your letter, with Mother's, yesterday. The paper had come in tonight when I got up, and Mother's card I got this morning when I came in from a walk.

So far I have felt much better for my holiday and have not been too tired to go out a little. Am still doing night duty as sister is off ill. It is a little cold here but when the sun gets out in the daytime it is soon hot. Am glad you are getting on in the garden. Miss Hancock – a Dr. here – is going home soon to be married; she said someone had told her they thought the war would end quite suddenly, so I thought of Mr. Sheldon's "collapse".[1]

There have been four deaths here since we came back. A boy, 23, had his foot off this morning – he was wounded near Loos in the big advance,[2] and a man tonight had his leg amputated. We do not hear much war news, but an officer said they would soon be settling down for the winter.

W.B.L. Mab.

1. Mr. Sheldon was a Deepcar worthy who came to play billiards with Mabel's father in the evenings. Like many people with a position to maintain, he had opinions about the war which he felt deserving of widespread propagation; his "collapse" theory was a popular but ill-informed one.

2. The Battle of Loos, 25 September–15 October 1915, was only a temporary advance for the Allies.

Royaumont. November 3rd, 1915, 4 a.m.

Dearest Mother,
I think I have had all your letters.

We had a pheasant for our dinner yesterday but it was very tough. One sister upset the coffee all over me, trying to get it off the bones.

In the woods one day I saw some deer, perhaps the meat is venison which is so tender here. There are pheasants in the grounds here.

This was where we used to sleep. It is now a ward called "Elsie Inglis".[1]

1. The creator of the Scottish Women's Hospitals Units; see Appendix B.

ASNIERES-sur-OISE

Edition de l'Épicerie Londière-Vibert L'h. Paris

PATRIE FAMILLE

15.12.15 Wed. night. 10.30 p.m.

Thank you very much for the *Queen*. You should really not have troubled to send me a Xmas parcel. I do hope you will take 10/6 for the shoes you gave me, I will ask Father to give it you out of my salary, also if you buy me a silk handkerchief you must take for that too.

Please will you get "*The Queen's Gift Book*" for you and Father for Xmas if you would like it, and everything for the others that you think they would like. My December salary will do for everything. It is cold here now. Best love.

Mab.

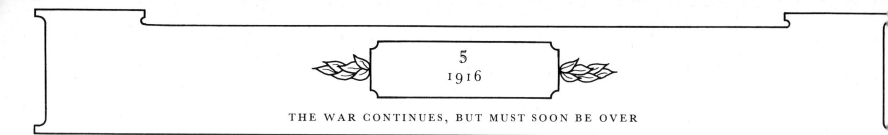
Sunday, January 2nd, 1916

Dearest Mother,

Thank you very much for your nice letter this morning and also for the second silk handkerchief which will be very useful. Am glad you all had a nice Xmas. I had this a.m. one half dozen handkerchiefs from Mrs. Holroyd, also a note to say there is a parcel for me at Viarmes station. I think it is from you.

Sister Harker and I had two days off and walked to Chantilly and stayed the night there; just opposite was the Hotel Condé where General Joffre and his staff are. We went through the Château, there were 500 or 600 Germans sleeping there last September year.

I do not want to stay here much longer, but perhaps might work somewhere else for a little time before coming home. Do you think the war is any nearer the end?

With best love to Father and you, Mabel.

1. The zouaves were a body of Algerian light infantry composed of French soldiers in oriental uniform.

ZOUAVES AT A GENERAL HALT[1]

9.1.16 Royaumont, Sunday night (*card not shown*)

My dear Father and Mother,
The hamper arrived here last night. Thank you very much. The cakes are lovely, we had some and the mince pies with a cup of tea yesterday and again today. The chocolate is very nice also. One of the sisters said the cake was the nicest she had ever tasted.
   It is frosty here tonight. The mince pies had broken very much, Mother, but everything was very nice.
   W.B.L. and M.T. from Mabel

21.1.16 (*card not shown*)

... The *Queen* you mention has not come yet but perhaps it will tomorrow. I have got as far as where Osbert goes down the mine after Gerald. I am still on night special – the man is much better. Is Adeline better now?

IN MEMORIAM

In the midst of this time of stress and strife
We mark the end of a peaceful life.
Filled to o'erflowing with loving deeds
With selfless efforts for others' needs.

No mourning crowd with its black array,
But our workaday garb of blue and grey,
As we troop in silence o'er the crest
Of the hill to take her away to rest.

A simple service of praise and prayer,
The notes of a hymn in the open air,
Her country's flag, white flowers and green,
Tokens of thanks for the life that has been.

The thunder of guns comes over the hill,
As we march away from the churchyard still,
With lifted faces, yet hearts bereft –
Carry on in her footsteps
The work she's left.

For Miss Butler
Royaumont. January 27th, 1916

(*Poem from Auntie Mabel's notebook*)

Readers who sense an echo of Wilfrid Owen's war poem, *Anthem for Doomed Youth*, in the second stanza, should remember that Owen's poem was not written until at least 1917. We leave the possibility of Mabel's influence on Owen undiscussed.

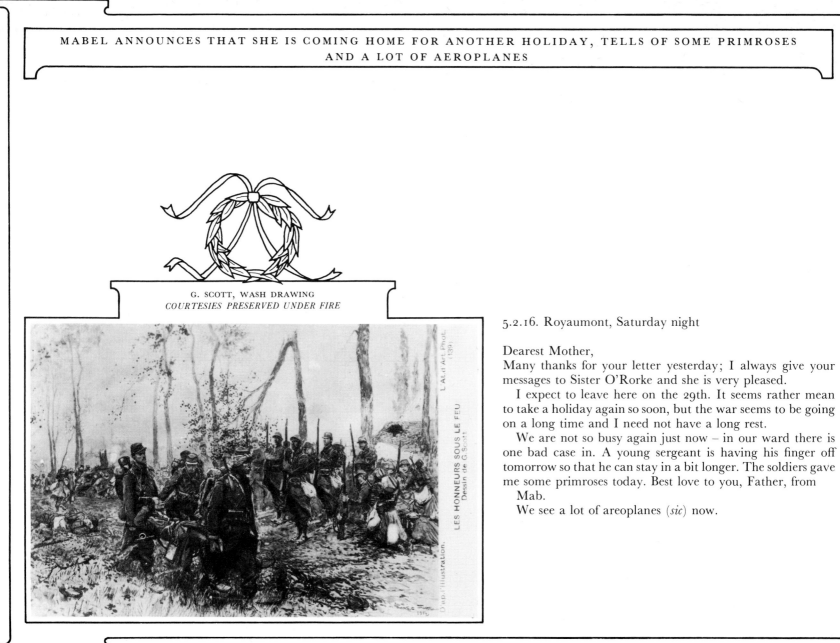

G. SCOTT, WASH DRAWING
COURTESIES PRESERVED UNDER FIRE

5.2.16. Royaumont, Saturday night

Dearest Mother,
Many thanks for your letter yesterday; I always give your messages to Sister O'Rorke and she is very pleased.

I expect to leave here on the 29th. It seems rather mean to take a holiday again so soon, but the war seems to be going on a long time and I need not have a long rest.

We are not so busy again just now – in our ward there is one bad case in. A young sergeant is having his finger off tomorrow so that he can stay in a bit longer. The soldiers gave me some primroses today. Best love to you, Father, from
Mab.

We see a lot of areoplanes (*sic*) now.

Ministère de la Guerre - Sté de secours aux Blessés Militaires - Croix Rouge Anglais

MINISTÈRE DE LA GUERRE.   **MINISTÈRE DE LA GUERRE**

Demi-tarif payable en 1re Classe

ORDRE DE TRANSPORT

Modèle A₁³.

POUR ISOLÉ SANS BAGAGES ET SANS CHEVAUX.

(Feuille de route.)

Nº 8 131631

(Voir au verso les observations importantes)

M. *Miss Jeffery Infirmière HOA de Royaumont*
(Nom et situation militaire de l'isolé.)

partant de — Corps ou Service expéditeur. *CMG*

Place de *CREIL*

à destination de — Corps ou Service destinataire. *CMG*

Place de *Boulogne s/ mer*

VISA A LA GARE DE DÉPART.

REÇU le bon de chemin de fer modèle A₁² portant le même numéro.

A _____ le *1er Mars* 19 16
    Le Chef de gare.

Timbre à date de la gare de départ

ITINÉRAIRE PAR VOIE FERRÉE.

De *CREIL* _____ *Boulogne s/ Mer*

à _____

par _____

AUTORITÉ QUI ÉTABLIT L'ORDRE DE TRANSPORT.

A _____ le *29 /2* 19 16
(Grade et signature.)

LE CAPITAINE

PARTIE A DÉTACHER POUR ÊTRE MISE A L'APPUI DES FEUILLES DE JOURNÉES OU DES REVUES D'OFFICIERS SANS TROUPE.

M. _____ partant de _____
   (Nom et situation militaire de l'isolé.)

le _____ pour se rendre à _____
   (Date du départ.)

Allocations de toute nature { perçues au départ _____

CERTIFIÉ EXACT

L'autorité qui établit l'ordre de transport, ou le Sous-Intendant militaire.

Le Titulaire.

M. E. Jeffery

Many such ambulances were required to collect the wounded from ports and stations and transfer them to hospitals.

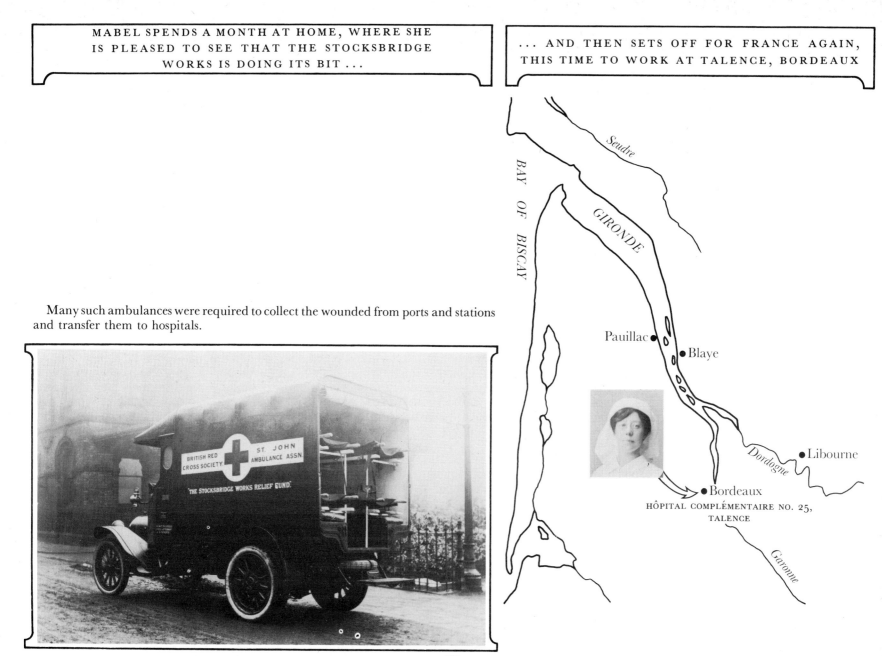

HÔPITAL COMPLÉMENTAIRE NO. 25,
TALENCE

56

La Guerre de 1914,
L. C. H. Paris

Les fameuses carrières de Soissons où étaient retranchés les Allemands
The famous quarries were the Germans were entrenched.

TALENCE — HÔPITAL COMPLÉMENTAIRE 25 — MAIN
ENTRANCE

Petit Lycée de TALENCE pendant la Guerre 1914-1915
TALENCE - Hôpital complémentaire N° 25 - Entrée principale   M. D

April 14th, 1916

Will post this when I get to Bordeaux, – it is about nine hours journey from Paris. The address is (Miss Gregory,) Hôpital Complémentaire 25, Talence, Gironde, which, they say, comes twenty-four hours sooner than if you put Bordeaux.

Will write later.

Hôpital Complémentaire 25,
Bordeaux,
Service Militaire
April 22nd, 1916

Hope you are having a nice Easter. Am waiting still to hear from you but expect it is scarcely time yet.[1] We heard an explosion today, – munition works blown up in Talence with many killed and injured. They say about 27 prisoners have come in here today. Now that the Russians have got into France perhaps *la guerre* will soon be over.[2]

Love from M.

1. This is probably a veiled reference to Mabel's sister's pregnancy, and the impending birth of Mrs. Turner, who arrived May 7th, 1916.
2. There were small numbers of Russian troops assisting the Allies in France, but Mabel may here misunderstand some additional action taken by the Tsar on behalf of France in late March, 1916. In an attempt to draw German troops away from Verdun, he intensified Eastern Front operations.

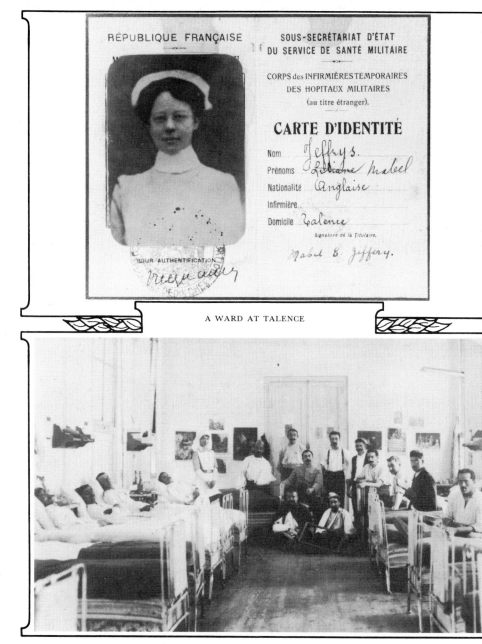

A WARD AT TALENCE

"The man in the chair is adjutant, he is nephew of one of the doctors here; he had both feet taken off."
(*Mabel on reverse*)

58

"The two black marks above the elbow show that he has been wounded twice."
(*Mabel on reverse*)

J.J. COUZE

CAPORAL LABBÉ MARCEL

JEAN BLANCHET

Bellan, Jean

(F) April 4th, 1916

241 Régiment Infanterie
5 Battaillon
PO Compagnie
1re Section
Secteur Postal No. 113

Please forgive my being so slow in writing to you to give you my news.

For the moment I am in perfect health and wish with all my heart that this card finds you the same. For the last few days we have had really fine weather, the sun is starting to be hot. When will this war end? The park at Royaumont must be lovely – do you still go in the boat. Nothing more to tell you at the moment. In expectation of good news I send you my greetings.

Bellan.

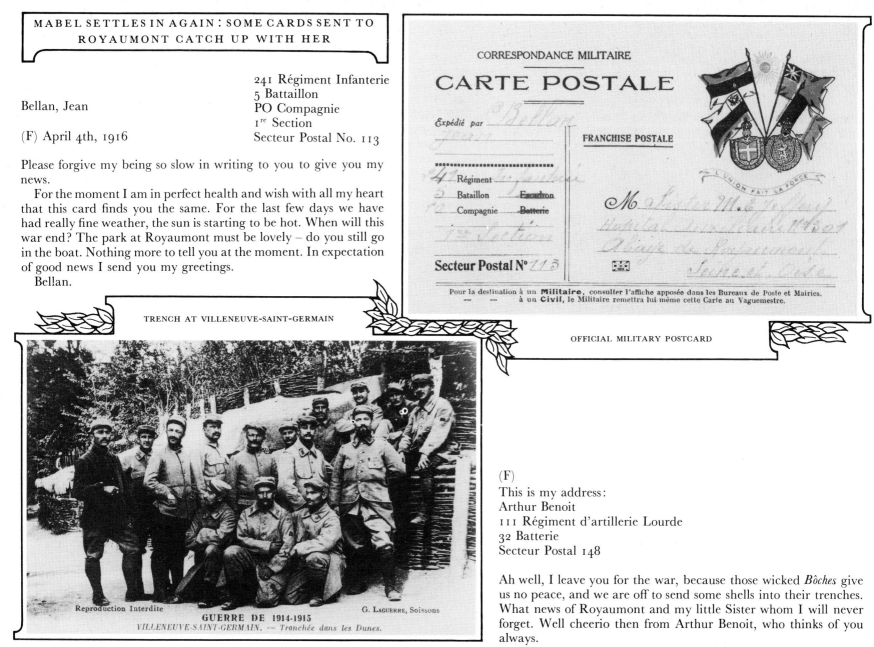

CORRESPONDANCE MILITAIRE

CARTE POSTALE

Expédié par

FRANCHISE POSTALE

Régiment
Bataillon   Escadron
Compagnie   Batterie

Secteur Postal Nº 113

Pour la destination à un **Militaire**, consulter l'affiche apposée dans les Bureaux de Poste et Mairies.
— à un **Civil**, le Militaire remettra lui-même cette Carte au Vaguemestre.

OFFICIAL MILITARY POSTCARD

TRENCH AT VILLENEUVE-SAINT-GERMAIN

Reproduction Interdite   G. LAGUERRE, Soissons
GUERRE DE 1914-1915
VILLENEUVE-SAINT-GERMAIN. — Tranchée dans les Dunes.

(F)
This is my address:
Arthur Benoit
111 Régiment d'artillerie Lourde
32 Batterie
Secteur Postal 148

Ah well, I leave you for the war, because those wicked *Bôches* give us no peace, and we are off to send some shells into their trenches. What news of Royaumont and my little Sister whom I will never forget. Well cheerio then from Arthur Benoit, who thinks of you always.

277. La Grande Guerre 1914-15 — *PARGNY-sur-SAULX - Bataille de la Marne - Les Allemands battus incendièrent la ville avant leur retraite*

THE GREAT WAR 1914–15 – PARGNY-SUR-SAULX – BATTLE OF THE MARNE – THE DEFEATED GERMANS SET FIRE TO THE TOWN BEFORE THEIR RETREAT

(F) April 14th, 1916

My dear little Sister
What great pleasure I take in giving you my news and in sending you this view of the war which will give you pleasure because I well know that Sister is very fond of views. I shall send several and I also send the great friendship Benoit has for Sister who cared for him so well when he was at Royaumont.

(F) June 5th, 1916

I send you these few words to give you my news, as also to ask for yours.[1]

I assure you that I am not lucky. I have just lost my wife, and find myself alone with my little girl; no one to help me any more, or to send me anything. I assure you that if it were not for the little one I should wish to die also, but for her I have to live. Let us hope that God will help me. I got your photograph, and I thank you very much for it. I think of you a lot, especially of the many favours you did me.

Nothing further to say for the moment. Goodbye and good health.

Bellan.

1. The postcard is of the same type as that used by Bellan opposite.

TRENCH OF THE BAYONETS

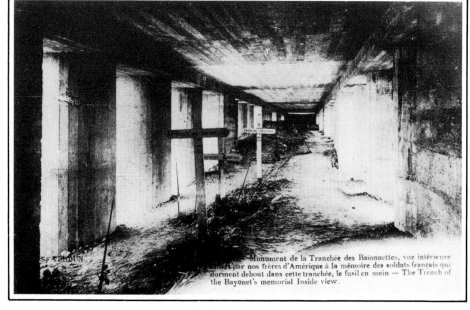

Monument de la Tranchée des Baïonnettes, vue intérieure ... par nos frères d'Amérique à la mémoire des soldats français qui dorment debout dans cette tranchée, le fusil en main — The Trench of the Bayonet's memorial Inside view.

There are 84 unknown French soldiers, who were waiting for the order to go "over the top"; a shell burst near them, their trench tumbled in and buried them all alive; the bayonets and guns are sticking out of the earth.

An American gentleman has put up the shelter of stone as a lasting memorial to them. (He himself was killed in an accident three days after he had given the money.)

"To the memory of the French soldiers unknown – who sleep under this trench – their guns in their hands."

(Mabel on reverse. The card was obtained by her at a later date.)

62

Fête
Talence Hôpital Militaire 25
July, 1916

This is a view of one of the Sunday fêtes given at Talence for the *blessés*. Have not had time to answer your letter but was very pleased to have it. The *Queen* would have come for 1d and if you have a *Girls Own Paper* to spare sometime would you send it. We are still enjoying the cakes and chocolates.

(*Mabel on reverse of photograph shown right*)

Sisters Morgan and Robinson, at Talence

Some enquiries about Sister Morgan received by Mabel, July–October, 1916, in the cards and letters opposite.

(F) – Dear Sister, you mention that Sister Morgan is leaving for Salonika; poor Sister travels too much. I saw last Sunday the news of the travellers who were coming from New York on the steamship Elysée, and there were three sisters: Miss Anna Morgan, Miss Elsie Aubury and Miss Wolfe. The ship arrived on Sunday evening at Bordeaux, but I'm quite sure that it wasn't Sister Morgan who went ashore to go on to Salonika, it is these rich travellers who wish to go all over the place and there are many other people called Morgan in England. –

(F) – You tell me that Sister Morgan sends her greetings. I thank you very warmly. What distresses me most is that she has to leave for Salonika. Will you try to get her address and let me know as soon as she arrives in Salonika. I thank you in advance for these little jobs I have given you, and which you will do for me. –

(F) – I hope you are having more luck than I; but I have at last received news of Sister Morgan, which makes me happy. –

(F) – Dear Sister, I do not forget you: I shall keep my promise about the ring as soon as I am able to leave. You would do me a great kindness if you would give me Sister Morgan's address, and when you write to Sister Robinson please greet her from me. –

(An unkind, if neatly contrived, cut)

Sisters: French, English, Irish, Scotch, Canadian, American, Welsh
Soldiers: French, Arabs, Singalese, Egyptian
(*Mabel on reverse*)

TAKEN AT TALENCE, 1916

WARD 11 AT TALENCE, JULY, 1916

Nurses of the French Flag Corps at Gradignan
in July, 1916

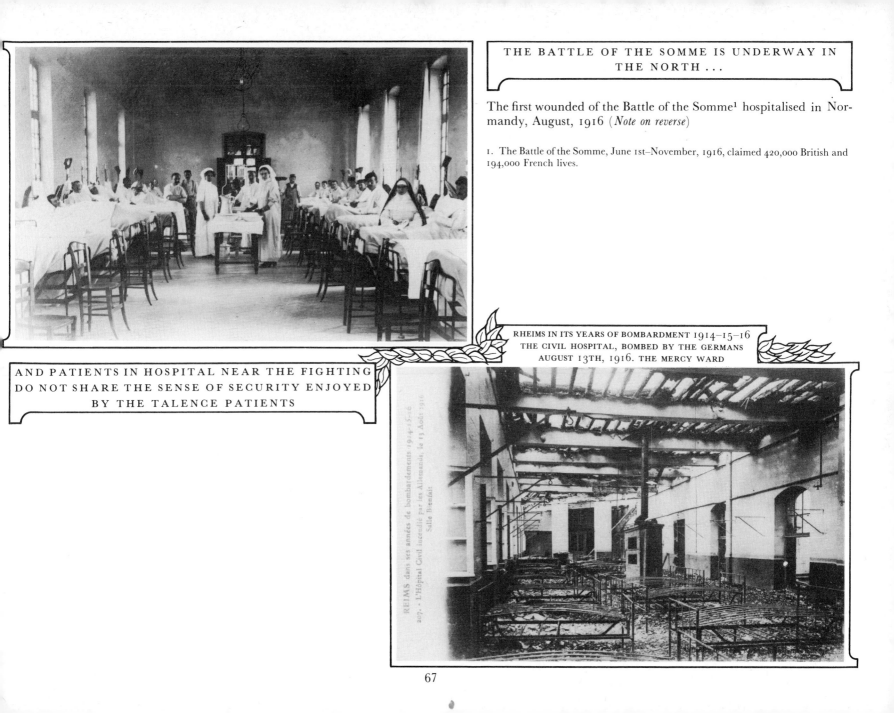

The first wounded of the Battle of the Somme[1] hospitalised in Normandy, August, 1916 (*Note on reverse*)

1. The Battle of the Somme, June 1st–November, 1916, claimed 420,000 British and 194,000 French lives.

AND PATIENTS IN HOSPITAL NEAR THE FIGHTING
DO NOT SHARE THE SENSE OF SECURITY ENJOYED
BY THE TALENCE PATIENTS

RHEIMS IN ITS YEARS OF BOMBARDMENT 1914–15–16
THE CIVIL HOSPITAL, BOMBED BY THE GERMANS
AUGUST 13TH, 1916. THE MERCY WARD

REIMS dans ses années de bombardements 1914-15-16
207.- L'Hôpital Civil incendié par les Allemands, le 13 Août 1916
Salle Bienfait

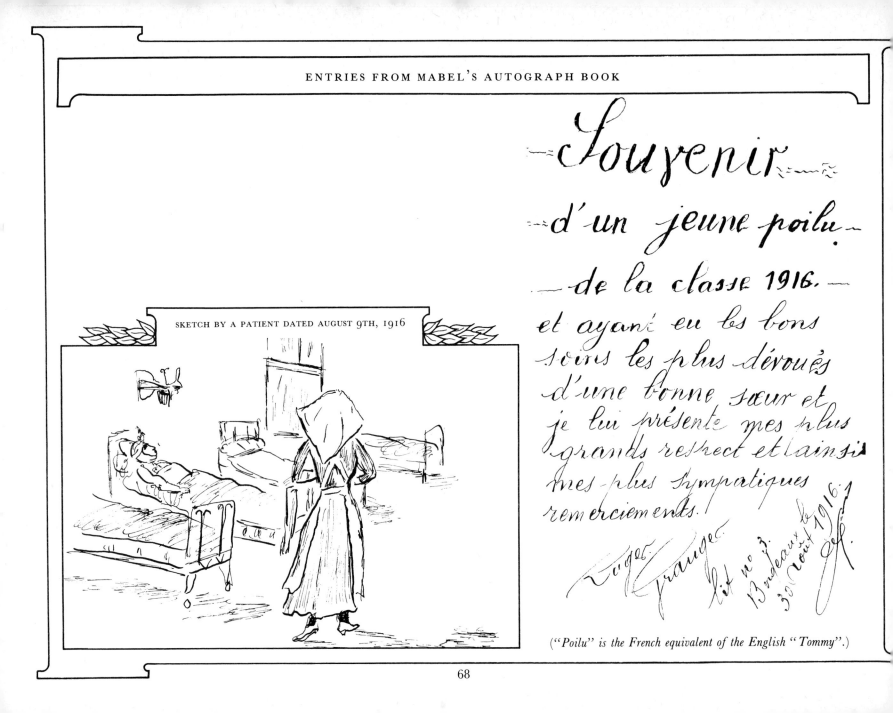

SKETCH BY A PATIENT DATED AUGUST 9TH, 1916

Souvenir

d'un jeune poilu.

de la classe 1916.
et ayant eu les bons
soins les plus dévoués
d'une bonne sœur et
je lui présente mes plus
grands respect et ainsi
mes plus sympatiques
remerciements.

Roger Granget.
lit no 3.
Bordeaux le 1916.
30 Aout 1916.

("Poilu" is the French equivalent of the English "Tommy".)

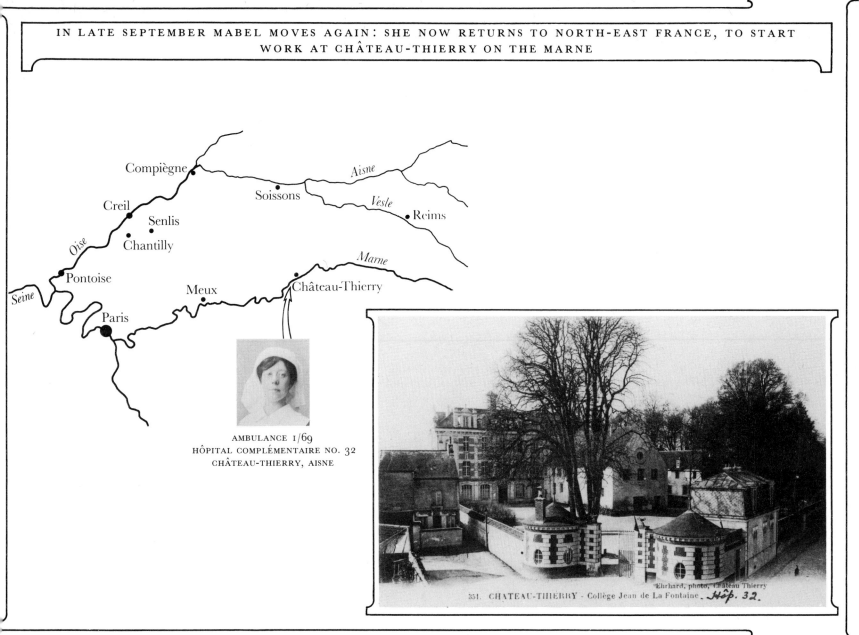

AMBULANCE 1/69
HÔPITAL COMPLÉMENTAIRE NO. 32
CHÂTEAU-THIERRY, AISNE

351. CHÂTEAU-THIERRY - Collège Jean de La Fontaine. *Hôp. 32.*

Ehrhard, photo, Château Thierry

MABEL'S STREET

57 CHATEAU-THIERRY — La Rue St-Martin

J. Bourgogne, éditeur, Château-Thierry

(*The following communication extends over the three cards on pp. 69, 70 and 75*)

68, Rue St. Martin,
Château-Thierry, Aisne
September 21st, 1916

Dearest Mother,

Very glad to have yours and one from Harry, today. They are only the second I have had here but the first time three came together. They say it took Miss Haswell five days to cross from England.

I am glad you will write to Sister Cannon as she was so very kind to me when I had my op.[1] Am sure she will be pleased as she has no Father and Mother on earth. I asked her if I should lend her my flea pads one day when she was very tired and said she was afraid she could not sleep for the fleas, but she said she did not like the smell of them and had really got a bit used to the fleas.

I gave her a little picture, Mother, in memory of her kindness to me and also of our work together in France, as we were in the same *service*.

The Doctor's name is "Pietri", and I wrote him a letter in English as Sister Naian said he liked that. He was very kind to me and came to see me the night after I had it done – as he was on guard, and also each day after until I got up, and then he said I could go to see him in the *Salle de Pansement*,[2] but not to go back on duty. When I asked him about it as I might have had to go away the next day after the op, he said he would do it for me but he would not let me go away for six or seven days and he would send a certificate.

I had worked hard for him Mother, and some of the cases especially had done very well I am glad to say. He was very pleased when his cases did well and very angry when they did not. One time he told me a man would die, but he did not.

This is a nerve-wracking place at night, someone has been throwing stones at my window but they have stopped now. Some officers are quartered opposite. On Saturday night a deserter was caught in the Rue St. Martin, climbing down our wall I think; we heard the shot, which was fired in the air. He has deserted 10 times from Champagne district, preferring, no doubt, prison to the trenches.

Have got a little present for the Baby,[3] but am afraid it may be sent back here – being in the war zone.

It is getting very cold. Am glad you liked Blackpool. Will ask for my leave soon now.

Best love from Mab.

1. Mabel had a minor operation before leaving Talence.
2. Dressings-theatre.
3. Mrs. Turner was now four months old.

If only I were big – (*Drawing by one of Mabel's patients*)

M. E. Jeffery, Ambulance 1/69, Secteur Postal 3
15.10.16

Leave Paris tomorrow night so may be home before this! There are rumours that all nurses may be recalled, but don't know if it is so.

(Original letter in English)

October 19th, 1916

Dear Miss,

Your departure has been so quick that I have not had the time to say you how I am thankful for all the cares you gave to me, for all the trouble I was the cause to you. I thank you very much for them and I will remember a long time your kindness towards me.

I am always at the ambulance. The throat-ache I've caught is not yet guarished,[1] and I have a very high fever: 40° yesterday evening! I'm not less a merry boy for that, but I can eat nothing and my legs begin again to be very feeble.

The major says he will send me when I shall be two days without having fever, but I don't know if I shall be strong enough for the travel after so short a time.

It's not so difficult to see you are gone away. Tables are not washed every day, nor the beds made! and I am obliged to ask it twenty times at the least, to have hot drinks or a dry shirt. Bah! We don't die for that. And Pasturel is now my "nurse", and a very clever and good one.

I hope your travel has been spent in a satisfying manner, and you have not been torpedoed, and also you have not been sea-sick.

I think I'll not remain here during a long time, now. It's wise, I think, to send at Auxi the letter I hope you'll soon write in answer.

Yours very thankful,
Paul Leleux
chez Madame A. Deselmont, Auxi-le-Château, Pas de Calais

---

1. Presumably "healed", derived from the French "*guéri*".

(French original with English postscript)

Dear Miss Jeffery,

I add my excuses to those of Number 2 (Leleux) and beg you to find herein my best thanks for the devoted care you have always lavished on me.

Nothing has changed regarding my departure which stays fixed for Sunday 22nd October, and I am happy to tell you that I have a month of convalescence.

With my reiterated thanks, believe me,
with respects,
Pasturel.

I am allways a notty boy.

Sergent Pasturel. 61: Infanterie   80 Route de Montpellier à Cette
Hérault

CARTE POSTALE

Le 28-10-16

I am always a

rotty boy.

Bons souvenirs et

hommages d'un de

vos anciens

malades

Pasturel

Sister

Broomfield

Deepcar

N. Sheffield

Angleterre

(LIME ... HERAULT postmark)

PASTUREL AND LELEUX

October 29th, 1916   (*Spelling of the English original retained in the letter below*)

Dear Miss,
I am yet in the ambulance, and I don't know how longer I'll remain yet. But I am now in another room, the "F3" and I have Miss Scott for my nurse. Its not so clean and not so merry as the pretty little room we occupied before, and I hop I will be here not a long time. It's forbidden to smoke and you know how I like to have beetwan my lips the mouthpies of my good old pipe. Happily I can now go out of my bed and I am used to walk in the yard backwards the house, smoking as an engine.

I have always a good remember of the weeks spent under your surveyance with my merry comrades. Pasturel has gone away on last Sunday, and now I know nobody to smile with him. Its very sad.

I hope you spend very happy holidays and you enjoy a very fine weather, finer than this of Château-Thierry where its always raining.

respectfully yours,
Paul Leleux

November, 1916

(left) Ward (*salle*) F1. at the Château-Thierry hospital, Ambulance 1/69.

(below left) Patients outdoors in the hospital courtyard

(below) Some of the Château-Thierry nursing staff in front of the *baraques*, temporary sheds which formed part of the hospital

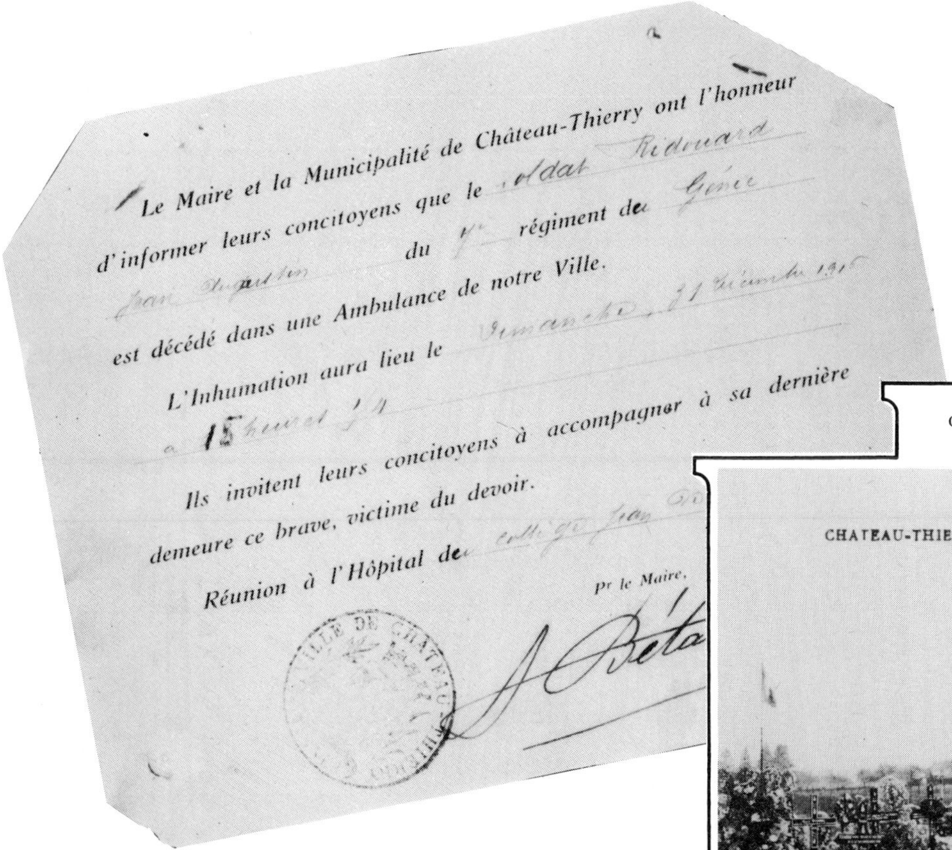

Le Maire et la Municipalité de Château-Thierry ont l'honneur d'informer leurs concitoyens que le soldat Ridouard Jean Augustin du 7e régiment du Génie est décédé dans une Ambulance de notre Ville.

L'Inhumation aura lieu le Dimanche, 21 décembre 1915 à 15 heures 1/4

Ils invitent leurs concitoyens à accompagner à sa dernière demeure ce brave, victime du devoir.

Réunion à l'Hôpital du collège Jean Ro

Pr le Maire,

A Béta

VILLE DE CHÂTEAU-THIERRY

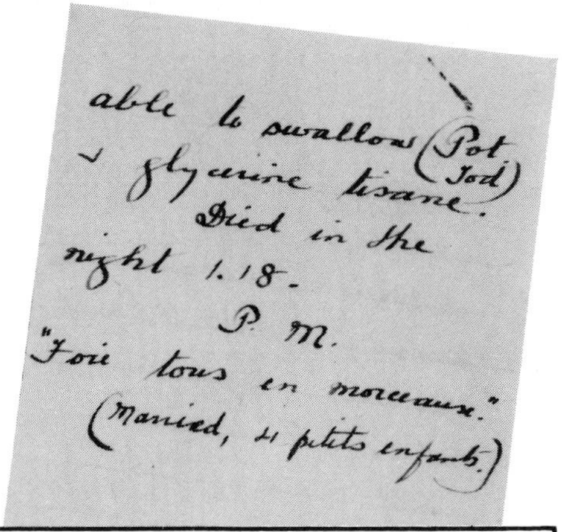

able to swallow (Pot Iod)
glycerine tisane.
Died in the night 1.18.
P. M.
"Foie tous en morceaux."
(Married, 4 petits enfants.)

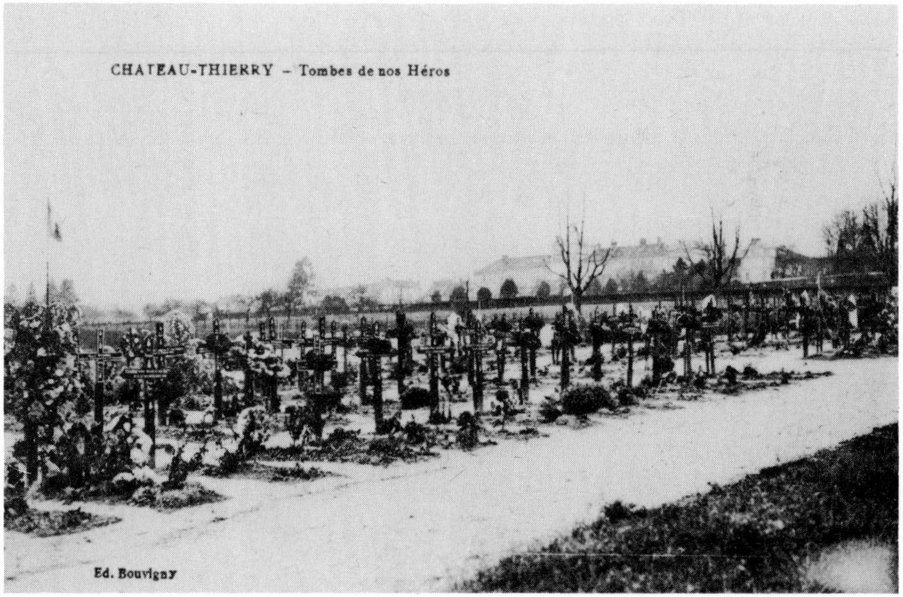

CHATEAU-THIERRY – Tombes de nos Héros
Ed. Bouvigny
CHÂTEAU-THIERRY – GRAVES OF OUR HEROES

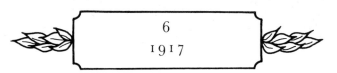

MABEL GETS NIGHT SOCKS AND AN APOLOGY . . .

IT'S FOR OUR SOLDIERS, LORD, I PRAY,
GOD GRANT MY PRAYERS AGAIN TODAY

*C'est pour nos soldats que j'implore
Exaucez-moi toujours, encore.*

jnhc
Editeur.Paris

518

55, Rue de la Madeleine
Sunday, January 7th, 1917

Many thanks for your last letter, also Father's. Please tell Father to mark his "Service Militaire" a little lower down, so that it can be seen after it has been opened and fastened up again by the censor. I hope you can read this – it is going all smudged. Very sorry to hear of Mrs. Haley's death. Don't send any more night socks, Mother, the others are lovely. We have just had some tea and cake. W.B.L.
    Mab.

(F) Paris, March 12th, 1917   *(card not shown)*

Dear Miss Jeffery,
All's well at this end; I found my family in good health. I hope I won't bore you, but I shall write to you from time to time when I have a moment.
    Dear Miss I would like to thank you for the time I had working with you; I was always in a temper, but please believe me it was not because of you, indeed I have never had any cause to be angry with you, and it would be very wrong of me because quite unmerited. Albeit I was not always in a good humour, if I was in a temper it was because the *service* was not running as I would have liked.
    Accept, Dear Miss Jeffery, the assurance of the good memories I keep of you; and I hope that when I work with a lady nurse again, it will be with one like yourself.
    L. Collet

1. L. Collet was a corporal (medical orderly) with Ambulance 1/69 – which had been based at Château-Thierry, but which was by now gone elsewhere, according to a postcard from Mabel not here reproduced.

THE TESTIMONY OF THE STONES

A card sold in aid of the wounded. Sent by an acquaintance who had just left Château-Thierry

(F) *undated*

Dear Sister,
I much regret not having said goodbye to you before leaving Château-Thierry. Because I was very busy the morning of my departure, with several last-minute preparations, I let you go off. It's to express my regrets about this that I write, and to tell you of the kind memories I retain of you, and I beg you to believe in the feeling of active sympathy that I ask you to convey also to Sister Rawlings and Sister Maize. Send my warmest congratulations to your dear country on the occasion of the entry into Baghdad,[1] and of the great success on the Ancre front – long live England.
    Let us hope for a rapid and definitive victory!
    Warmly yours, N. Ponsin

1. Baghdad fell on March 11th, 1917.

(F) *undated*

Dear Miss,
Just a few lines to give you my news. My leave was very good, but not long enough.
    Dear Miss, accept my best wishes,
    – your friend, Ernest Reès

CHÂLONS CAMP, THE MONOPLANE ANTOINETTE

LE CANAL
TOUR DU CONNÉTABLE
ROUTE DE NANTES
UN COIN
LE CHÂTEAU
LA FORÊT DU GÂVRE
SOUVENIR DE BLAIN
Artaud et Nozais, Nantes

This card, like the one from the same correspondent on the previous page, comes from a tear-out book sold in aid of the wounded.

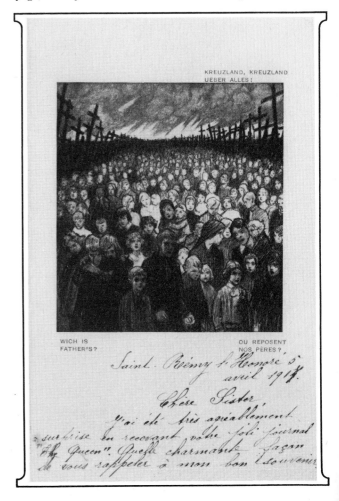

(F) Dear Miss,   March 23rd, 1917
Most happy to have got your news, and also to know that your ring has arrived alright. Dear Sister I promised it to you and I have kept my promise. I have constantly a thought for you, because you have looked after me as if you were our mother. I congratulate you on your bravery and the devotion you show towards the sick. The English do very well on the Somme. Long live our allies. Dear Sister I will finish now. Accept my warm greetings: your *grand malade* from ward II (Talence).
(*on front*) Where I am billeted – the château
    Pacard Auguste

    Dear Sister,   April, 1917
I was pleasantly surprised to receive your nice magazine "The Queen". What a charming way for you to send me your remembrances. Certainly I could not forget what a very likable person you are. I thank you from the bottom of my heart for your gesture of friendship, and send you my most friendly greetings.
    Warmly Yours, N. Ponsin.

(*card below*) M. Carpentier, like M. Collet, worked with Ambulance 1/69 and moved with it when it left the hospital at Château-Thierry.

> Dear Miss Jeffery. Since I met you at Ch.^au, new things have happened. We left the small country where we were at rest last Saturday. and we took succession of an active formation at the rear of the front. Much noise here, but less work for us. we are cleaning the hospital and evacuating the patients preparing for surgery. the English soldiers are now making good work. Hurrah. Friendly yours
>
> 19. April 1917   D. Carpentier

17   CATHÉDRALE DE SÉES. — Le Chœur.   ND. Phot.

(*English original*) 19.4.17

Miss,

My travel has been excellent. But I was a little tired ... To-day at home, in my room, I am happy.

Thank you very much for your devotedness and for your amability. You have supposed that I was "a grandfather" because my beard. No, miss! – *I am a catholic priest, vicar at cathedral of Sées* (*Orne*).

Again thank you and God save you!

Ed. Vaucaun

(Room F2, bed 7)

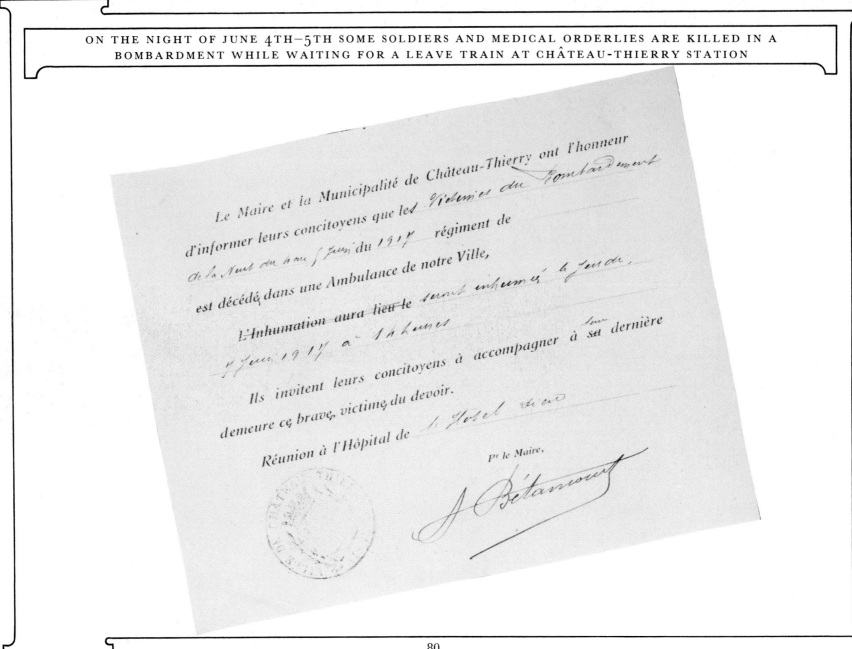

Le Maire et la Municipalité de Château-Thierry ont l'honneur

d'informer leurs concitoyens que les *Victimes du Bombardement*

de la Nuit du 4 au 5 Juin du 1917 régiment de

est décédé dans une Ambulance de notre Ville,

L'Inhumation aura lieu le *seront inhumés le Jeudi*

7 Juin 1917 à *14 heures*

Ils invitent leurs concitoyens à accompagner à *leur* dernière

demeure ce brave, *victimes* du devoir.

Réunion à l'Hôpital de *l'Hôtel Dieu*

Pr le Maire,

J. Bétancourt

(F)
Memento of the poor soldiers who were victims of the *Boche* assassins.
5th June 1917

2 medical orderlies, 11 soldiers killed in the night of 4th–5th June at the station at Château-Thierry by the *Boches'* bombs.

All these victims were leaving for 7 days home leave.

May God punish these infamous brigands.
(*note written on the back of the funeral invitation opposite*)

June 12th, 1917

Dearest Mother,
Very many thanks for the tea today, you are really too kind and good to me. Madame seems to enjoy her cups of tea so much, but I think perhaps it is the attention she likes. Her own daughter is too tiresome to live at home – she has had to be sent away. Madame is quite well off so I cannot give her money as I could to a poor person.

It is so quiet here now that perhaps I could get home for my leave, but the awkward part is we never know when the work will come in, and you will understand it is rather difficult to get away. This is where the damage was done by the bombs.

Heaps of love. Shall I send Father a bottle of hair lotion, your hair is so pretty now you would not need it. Many thanks.
    Mab.

CHÂTEAU-THIERRY – THE STATION

CHÂTEAU-THIERRY. — *Vue sur la Gare.*   ND. *Phot.*

THE SCENE OF THE CRIME BEFORE IT HAPPENED

LE GRAND EMPEREUR

6 LA ROCHE-sur-YON (Vendée)

Le Grand Empereur

Artaud et Nozals, Nantes

(*Original letter in English*)
June 16th, 1917

Dear Miss,
Next time I went to Château-Thierry I did not find the time to visit you at the hospital. I was rather busy and disposed of few hours.

We still stay in the same country at our huge field hospital of 3800 beds. We have very little work and we should be extremely satisfied to fly anywhere else, especially in Alsace. We here fight against two enemies – the sun and the mousquitoes. Also – the air-craft pills. Recently two non explosed shells and a aircraft bomb fell among our *baraques* – and some of our boys were wounded – especially *maréchal des logis*[1] Pottier who has been operated and since evacuated. We know you are exposed to same inconvenients. I hope you are not to see them quite near.

Always happy to hear of our former hospital. I send you my best regards
D. P. Carpentier
Amb 1/69, S.P.102

(F) La Roche-sur-Yon
July 4th, 1917

Dear Sister,
Very happy to have your news, I hasten to answer you. I'm sure that I shall *never* forget you, because you have been so kind to me. You will forgive my being a little slow in answering as I got your kind letter on returning from seven days leave, and I see that you in your turn are going off. That's very good. I wish you a good journey.

I have not received any news from Sister Morgan.

My best regards, Pacard Auguste

1. The sergeant-in-charge.

MABEL'S PARIS ITINERARY

Permit Office
18, Rue Chauveau Lagarde
Consulat
6, Rue Montalivet

Métro – to Cité –
Prefecture
Quai aux Fleurs
July 5th, 1917

1st, Permit Office *with* passport – not far from Gare St. Lazare

2nd, *Consulat* 6 Rue Montalivet (about 7 minutes walk)
Métro to Cité. Prefecture just across the road
Métro, again to Gare St. Lazare.
Grand Hôtel du Havre
(side street) (4 francs for room)

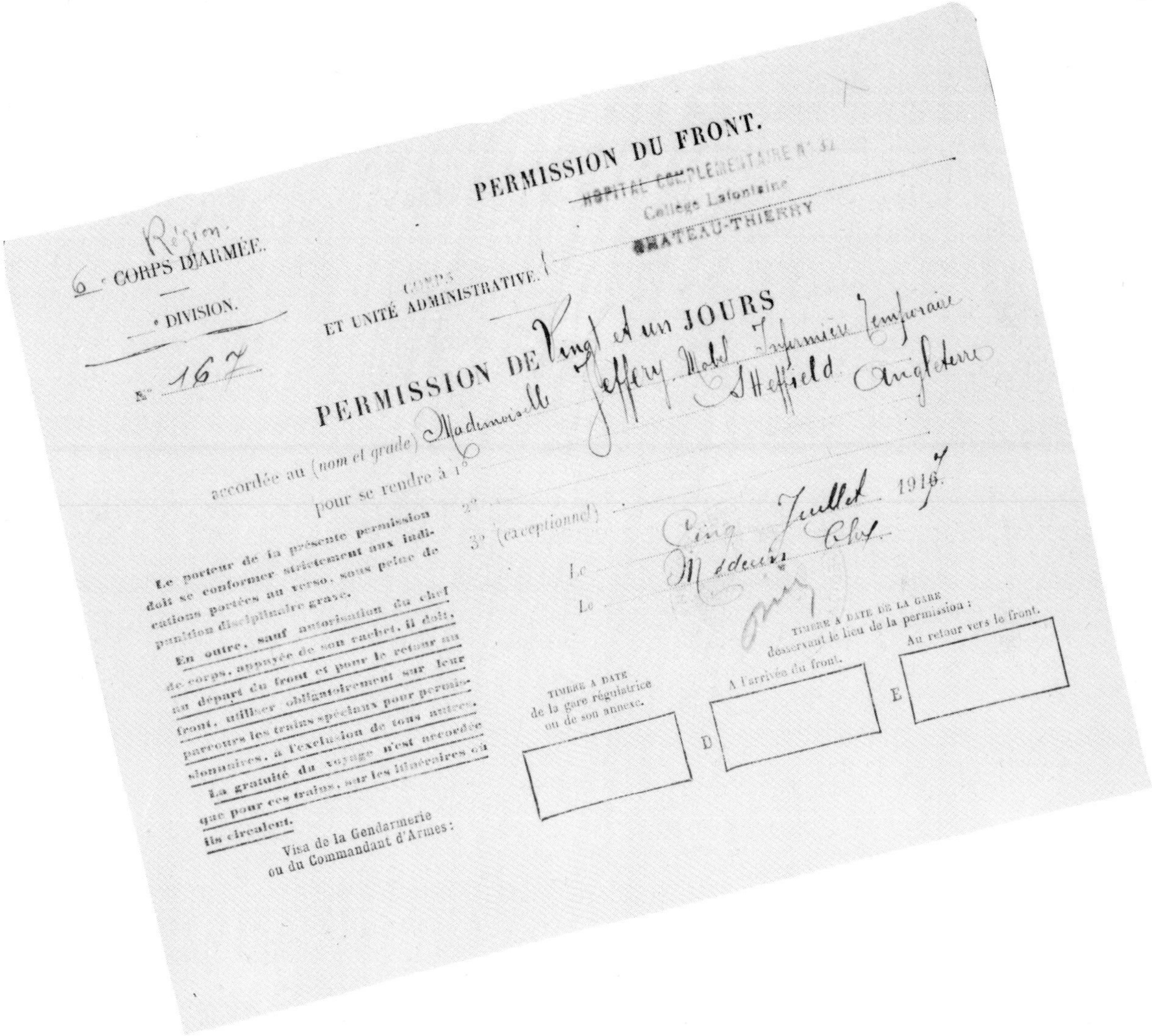

Région
6ᵉ CORPS D'ARMÉE.
ᵉ DIVISION.
Nº 167

PERMISSION DU FRONT.

CORPS ET UNITÉ ADMINISTRATIVE. HOPITAL COMPLÉMENTAIRE Nº 32 Collège Lafontaine CHATEAU-THIERRY

PERMISSION DE Vingt et un JOURS

accordée au (*nom et grade*) Mademoiselle Jeffery Mabel Infirmière Temporaire

pour se rendre à 1º Sheffield Angleterre

2º

3º (*exceptionnel*)

Le Cinq Juillet 1917.

Le Médecin Chef.

Le porteur de la présente permission doit se conformer strictement aux indications portées au verso, sous peine de punition disciplinaire grave.

En outre, sauf autorisation du chef de corps, appuyée de son cachet, il doit, au départ du front et pour le retour au front, utiliser obligatoirement sur leur parcours les trains spéciaux pour permissionnaires, à l'exclusion de tous autres.

La gratuité du voyage n'est accordée que pour ces trains, sur les itinéraires où ils circulent.

Visa de la Gendarmerie ou du Commandant d'Armes:

TIMBRE A DATE de la gare régulatrice ou de son annexe.

D

TIMBRE A DATE DE LA GARE desservant le lieu de la permission :
A l'arrivée du front.

E

Au retour vers le front.

(*Original letter in English*)
Château-Thierry
July 9th, 1917

Dear Miss Jeffery,
I was very happy to receive your nice card, and I hope your travel was quite good.

I am very satisfied with the hospital. You were so good to show me every thing that I was no "losed" like I was afraid.

I have good news to give you from all our soldiers.

The *typhoïque*[1] is much better he had 36°9 this morning and will eat an egg to dinner. The others are well, some of them will go on this week.

Sergeant Peters is very good, he helps me in every thing and the *infirmiers* also.

Miss Maize, Miss Willing came to see me and ask to help me, but you show me every part, so well, it was not useful.

I hope, dear Miss Jeffery you are happy at home.

Thank you very much to think about me, you are so good!

Excuse me for my bad English. I am quite ashamed to send you so ugly letter.

I am, dear Miss Jeffery, your very affectionately,
Suzanne Nusse

The green plant is very well.

1. Typhoid patient.

(CENSORED) THE CHÂTEAU GATE
(TURNED INTO AN *AMBULANCE* HOSPITAL)[1]

Grille du Château
(transformé en ambulance)

Ambulance: 12/14
Secteur: 181
September 21st, 1917

Dear Miss Jeffery,
This is only a line to send you my love – we have no time for anything. Willets and I are taking turns of sitting up at night, *part* of the night at least – I doubt if the man will live after all. We love to have your news. We miss you and all the dear people at Château-Thierry, but it is very pleasant here. I could say a lot more, but daren't. We are in *such* hot water with the authorities.
    Love from Mac[2]

1. This was probably Vauxbuin, near Soissons, where Ambulance 12/14 was to be found shortly after.
2. Sister Maxwell, who worked with Mabel at Royaumont before going on to La Panne (p. 34).

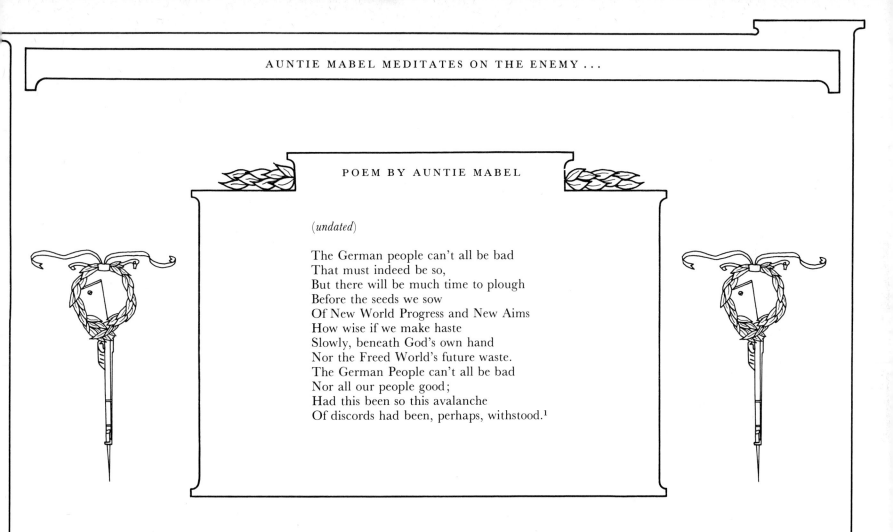

POEM BY AUNTIE MABEL

(undated)

The German people can't all be bad
That must indeed be so,
But there will be much time to plough
Before the seeds we sow
Of New World Progress and New Aims
How wise if we make haste
Slowly, beneath God's own hand
Nor the Freed World's future waste.
The German People can't all be bad
Nor all our people good;
Had this been so this avalanche
Of discords had been, perhaps, withstood.[1]

1. Like most of Mabel's poems this is undatable, as her style remained substantially unchanged over forty years, and the palimpsest nature of her notebooks does not help. It is well perhaps to regard this as a draft for a poem which was never returned to, as the versification does not exhibit Mabel's usual fastidiousness. In particular line 7 seems to lack a monosyllable, and the last two lines seem quite unresolved, only the substance of the thought and the end rhyme having been formulated.

"Château-Thierry Oct. 17, 1917, *killed*"
(*Mabel on reverse*)[1]

"They said this was the officer's brother and mother. I have several others."
(*Mabel on reverse*)

These four photographs seem to have been taken from the German officer in the first picture whose name would therefore be Otfried Sander, and who, according to the inscription on the back, was killed on October 17th, 1917. The next picture is "said to be of his mother and brother", and the last is from a brother (Helmut) who is clearly not the brother in the second photograph. Whether the Albrecht who sent the third photograph, and presumably appears in it, is the brother of the second photograph, another brother, or just a friend, it is not possible to decide.

The second, third and fourth pictures have pin-holes in the corners which seem to indicate that the officer had had them (though not of course his own picture) pinned up in his barracks or reserve-line dug-out, but had put them in his pocket for active duty. [M. W., J. C.]

1. The photographs on this page come from the studio of H. Noack, Hofphotograph, Berlin, Unter den Linden 54–55 and Bayrischer Platz 2.

ALBRECHT

(*Text reads, translated from German:*)
My Dear Otfried
as a souvenir of the Argonnes[1]
   Albrecht
   Officers' Dug-out, position 513
   May, 1917

(*Text reads, translated from German:*)
2nd Hanoverian Lancers, 14
I Squadron
Imperial German Field
Mail Service
29.1.17   3–4p.m.
199 Infantry Division
to:
Leutenant
O. Sander 2nd Class
5th Battery
Imperial Field Artillery
Regiment 43
V Imperial Army Corps

28.1.17
My dear Otfried![2]
Still no news from you. Haven't
you had any letters from me at all?
This picture is of the entrance to
my dug-out with my Adjutant and
Möppel[3] between his legs.
With heartfelt greetings from your
brother Helmut

HELMUT

1. The Argonnes are a wooded area
of north-east France.

2. Perhaps Otfried, as an artillery officer
operating in the Château-Thierry district
in the autumn of 1917, was responsible for
the bombardment which is the subject of
pages 80 and 81.

3. German colloquialism for a pug-like
dog.

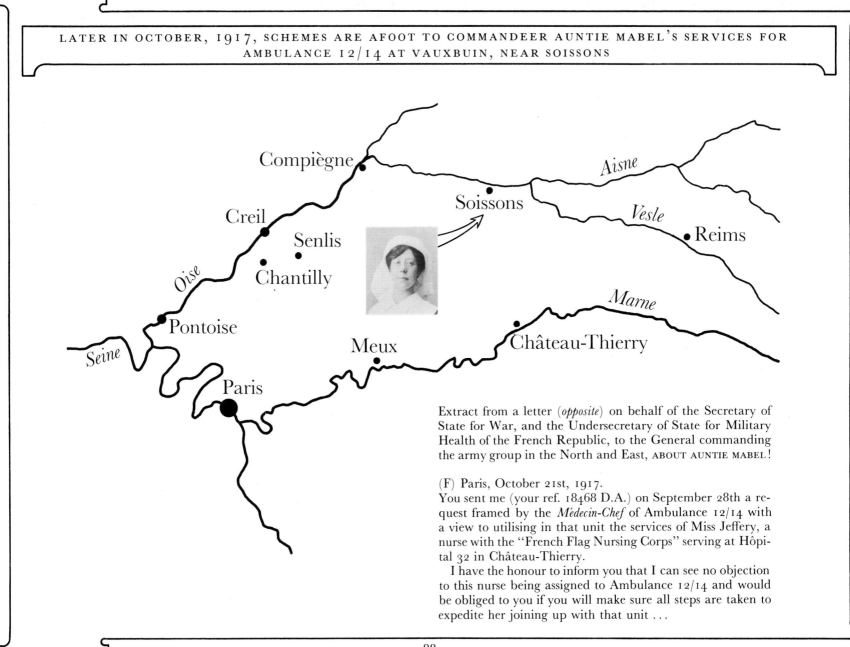

Compiègne

Aisne

Creil

Soissons

Vesle

Senlis

Reims

Chantilly

Oise

Marne

Pontoise

Meux

Château-Thierry

Seine

Paris

Extract from a letter (*opposite*) on behalf of the Secretary of State for War, and the Undersecretary of State for Military Health of the French Republic, to the General commanding the army group in the North and East, ABOUT AUNTIE MABEL!

(F) Paris, October 21st, 1917.
You sent me (your ref. 18468 D.A.) on September 28th a request framed by the *Médecin-Chef* of Ambulance 12/14 with a view to utilising in that unit the services of Miss Jeffery, a nurse with the "French Flag Nursing Corps" serving at Hôpital 32 in Château-Thierry.

I have the honour to inform you that I can see no objection to this nurse being assigned to Ambulance 12/14 and would be obliged to you if you will make sure all steps are taken to expedite her joining up with that unit ...

ORDRE DE TRANSPORT
POUR ISOLÉ SANS BAGAGES ET SANS CHEVAUX
(Feuille de route)
(Voir au verso les observations importantes)

Modèle **A_i³**.

M. Jefferies, Infirmier,

partant de — Corps ou Service expéditeur — Hôpi...
Place de

à destination de — Corps ou Service destinataire
Place de

ITINÉRAIRE PAR...
De — Château
à — St. Christophe
par — Paris

PARTIE A DÉTACHER POUR ÊTRE MISE A L'A...
M.
le
(Nom et situation militaire de l'isolé)
(Date de départ)
Allocations de toute nature perçues au départ

L'Autorité qui établit l'ordre de transport ou le Sous-Inten...

MINISTÈRE DE LA GUERRE

République Française

Paris le 21 octobre 1917

Ministère de la Guerre
Sous-Secrétariat d'État
au Service de Santé Militaire
1ʳᵉ Division technique

N° 23944 2/7

A.S. de Mlle Jefferies
de nationalité anglaise

Le Sous-Secrétaire d'État du
Service de Santé Militaire à Monsieur
le Général Commandant en Chef le
groupe d'Armées du Nord et de l'Est

Vous m'avez transmis sous le N° 18468 D.A. à
la date du 28 Septembre une demande formée par M. le
Médecin Chef de l'Ambulance 1/51 en vue d'utiliser dans cette
formation les services de Mlle Jefferies, infirmière du « French
Flag Nursing » corps en service à l'Hôpital 32 à Château Thierry.
... j'ai l'honneur de vous faire connaître que...

(F)
to Miss Jeffery, Sister
Ambulance 12/14
Secteur Postal 181
November 19th, 1917

In answer to your card which I got a few days ago. I am very happy that you have done so well; and that you are well pleased and above all that you tell me all is very pleasant. I see that you are happy with your move. You ask me what I have been up to. I am still more than enough with my ladies; Madeleine has been replaced and is at A2 with Mlle. Suzanne. Now in the B wards we have four male nurses, counting Parail, and beyond those three ladies, counting Mlle. Plue, and wouldn't that make it seem that the *service* should be better than usual: actually it is to the contrary.

A circular came two days ago, and there is a strong rumour that we are going to leave for Salonika. What a jolly trip that will be.

Rocher
Your *infirmier* who misses you.

Extract from text: (F)
... My best wishes for the year's end. Let us hope that the one about to begin will see the end of this dreadful war. I wish you a "Good Christmas" (English) ...

FEBRUARY: MABEL'S CARDS ARE CENSORED. THE GERMANS MAKE A FINAL DRIVE

Ambulance 12/14, S.P. 181, 21.2.18

Many thanks for letter yesterday of February 11. Sometimes now the new postman brings them up in the afternoon. Am already counting up the time for July and the little Sergeant Major says he is hoping to spend ten days with us if he can get his permission. Hope you are keeping well, also Father. Are you and Evelyn busy?[1]

1. Evelyn or "Evie" was the maid. Although written from Vauxbuin, this card bears a view of one of the bridges at Château-Thierry. Its caption has been removed by the censor.

(F)
Bar-le-Duc – Meuse
April 17th, 1918

My Dear Sister,
I send you these few lines to give you my news and to ask you to send yours as I haven't heard from you for a long time. As for me I left Château-Thierry on February 12th, and as of this moment I am working as a cook. I am in good health, but I'm waiting for the end. In your last letter you were saying that wouldn't be long; I believe so too, but I see that it hasn't finished yet. When you answer you will tell me what you think. I think that at the moment the English are having difficulty holding on and I think that that must be terrible in the face of such a force. I am in good health and I wish you the same.

Your devoted friend, Julien Rocher

THE GREAT WAR 1914–18. AERIAL BOMBARDMENT AT BAR-LE-DUC, MAISON PELEGRIN, QUAI VICTOR HUGO

(CENSORED) – THE ENTRANCE TO THE FOREST.
THE CALVARY

Entrée de la Forêt. Le Calvaire.

Ambulance 12/14,
S.P. 181,
le 10 mai, 1918

Dearest Mother,
Many thanks for yours today, dated April 27th – you had addressed S.P. 141, so perhaps that delayed it some. Thanks for notice of change of address,[1] it will do to send on to the Corps Headquarters. Am not so busy yesterday and today. It is still close but does not altogether clear up. Hope your cold is well now.

    Love from Mab.

(*censored*) is where the Royaumont people began another hospital[2]

1. Mabel's parents at this time moved from their house "Broomfield", in Deepcar, to "Moor Cliff", in Sheffield.
2. The picture is of the forest of Villiers-Cotteret, where the Scottish Women's Hospitals Committee had set up another hospital.

This was to put us under the protection of the *Médecin-Chef* at V.C.[1] when we had to leave Soissons.[2] He asked for four *infirmières* to go and help at the Scottish Women's hospital there, after the raid at night, but we were all very tired, and four French women went.

(note on the back of the above)

1. Villiers-Cotteret; see opposite.
2. On May 29th, 1918, the Germans captured Soissons.

(translation by Mabel)

June 2nd, 1918

Dear Sister,

I send you my news which are not too bad, as I have just come back from leave. I have the "*caffard*" (fed-up) but I think that I have not more to complain than you, above all at this time, after all that had passed over your way. You are "evacuated" I think.

If you could see all the poor refugees everywhere – and they are right for it is not a sweet dream to stay behind for the *Bôches*[1] – what a terrible war all the same. When will it be finished. I hope that you, dear sister, are not any longer in danger. This is my wish for you.

Your old patient, Pacard Auguste

1. The French original describes the *Bôches* as "*maudits*" (damned); fastidious Mabel has left out this adjective in her translation.

22.6.18
Saturday night

chez Miss Haswell[1]
36 Rue Châteaudun, Paris 9ᵉ

Dearest Daddy,

Many thanks for yours of the 18th, just come in. Am sorry if I have neglected you but have written a good deal altogether. Many thanks for the news and many congrats. on the presents and especially on the way you are leaving your "regiment", which shows you are a "tried and trusted" member, – as Miss Haswell says about us if we are going on to pastures new.

We are to be ready for Monday – with photos – so expect we may be going back to the front, but we have had a very nice rest here.

Please give enclosed to Mother. W.B.L. Mab.

1. Miss Haswell was Matron in France of the French Flag Nursing Corps, a department of the French Red Cross in which British nurses worked.

4006. PARIS – Panorama pris de Notre-Dame

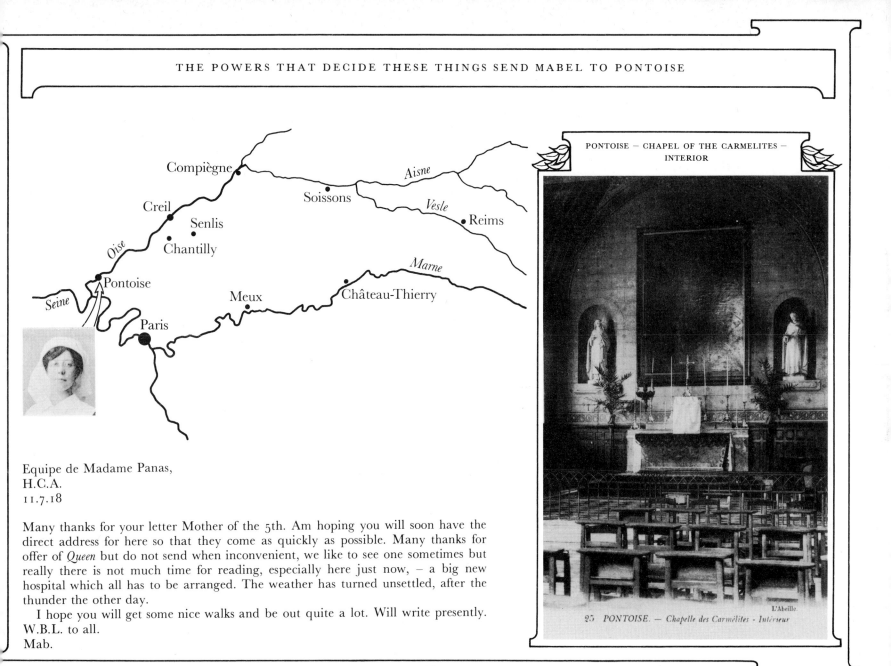

PONTOISE – CHAPEL OF THE CARMELITES – INTERIOR

25 PONTOISE. — Chapelle des Carmélites - Intérieur

Equipe de Madame Panas,
H.C.A.
11.7.18

Many thanks for your letter Mother of the 5th. Am hoping you will soon have the direct address for here so that they come as quickly as possible. Many thanks for offer of *Queen* but do not send when inconvenient, we like to see one sometimes but really there is not much time for reading, especially here just now, – a big new hospital which all has to be arranged. The weather has turned unsettled, after the thunder the other day.

   I hope you will get some nice walks and be out quite a lot. Will write presently. W.B.L. to all.
Mab.

VERS LA VICTOIRE

VERSAILLES, PETIT TRIANON, THE MILL

(F) Larëole. Monday, July 19th, 1918

Dear Sister
I hasten to answer your charming card; it gave me great pleasure to learn your good news. For the moment I am in the best of health, and I hope the present finds you in the same, dear Sister. I am very happy with the gift the operating theatre sister sent me; but when I am in Algeria one day, I shall not forget you. I am very happy and I remember you always, I do not forget you for a single moment and I will let you have my news whenever I can and I shall be very happy to receive yours.

Greetings to operating theatre sister Miller, to Miss Craig, to all the men in the ward – and accept the best wishes for your happiness.
Eugène Fernandez

July 25th, 1918

Thanks so much for your letters, we are still very busy, *blessés* come in by 100s every day.

How nice to get the strawberries, etc. from Broomfield.[1] Am afraid we did not appreciate the rhubarb enough.
W.B.L.   Mab.

1. These must have been preserved at Broomfield before the move to Moor Cliff.

96

(F) David Albin 143 Inf. Hôp. 110. Val-André, Cot. du Nord (*undated*)

Miss

A secret: the war will be over for Christmas. Yes! It's true – The hospital here by the sea isn't too bad! But the nurses aren't as nice as at Pontoise. ▶

    My respects –

July 27th, 1918

Dearest Mother,

Have always forgotten to tell you that we buy saccahrin (*sic*) here – as there is not much sugar.[1] If you put in very, *very* little, it sweetens rather nicely, but too much is very nasty, – *not more* than $\frac{1}{2}$ a tiny tabloid for a *big* cup of tea.

    My stockings – white ones – are in big holes but the legs are good, I wonder if I could wear two pairs of them – I have some silk ones?

    W.B.L. Mab.

1. Sugar, which had been imported from Germany, was in short supply in Britain towards the end of the war.

LA BRETAGNE PITTORESQUE
9330 — Val-André - *La Plage, côté Sud*

THE VIOSNE AT PONTOISE

11. Pontoise Pittoresque — *Les Bords de la Viosne - Lavoir*

H.C.A. Pontoise
25.8.18

This is a view of our hospital but it is much bigger now – I work in the "*pavaillon*" standing across and Miss Wood and I sleep in a room marked – on the left. The cars bring in the *blessés* into the courtyard – now there is a big tent there – the "*salle de tirage*", with all the *salles d'opération* leading off. They come in practically every day and night. We have Italian stretcher-bearers who wander about wondering where to take the men. It is my night on duty. Hope you are all well.
    W.B.L. Mab.

PONTOISE – THE BARRACKS – INNER COURTYARD

3.8.18, Saturday night (*card not shown*)

Dearest Mother,
Thanks so much for the white stocking, it is so pretty, but I did not mean I wanted any more, only it seems such a pity when the feet are worn out and the legs are good.
    Fancy Soissons being ours again.

October 13th, 1918

Dearest Daddy,
Many thanks for your letter today of the 7th. I posted one to you and Mother this morning but it was an awful scribble; we are busy now because so many have left. My photo is not on this card yet but I hope soon to be amongst the crowd, however they all say the end will be very soon now and I am sure I shall like the house, whatever the weather.
  Much love. Mab.

LEAVE TRAINS

LES TRAINS DE PERMISSIONNAIRES.

696 A.N PARIS

D'après l'illustration   par L. Sabattier.

SOISSONS — Intérieur de la Cathédrale

October 13th, 1918

Dearest Mother,
I wrote last night on purpose to say how sorry I was you had been feeling tired, and I finished up the letter without mentioning it! I hope you are better now. The English paper you sent me is very interesting. I will write to Evelyn soon.
  W.B.L. Mab.

Les Alliés à 8 kilomètres DE BRUGES

Cinq mille habitants de Courtrai ont été délivrés

A la Statue de Lille

PLACE DE LA CONCORDE

A la statue de Lille des drapeaux sont mêlangés aux gerbes de fleurs et de couronnes. On remarque beaucoup de lauriers et une palme de lauriers déposée par les soins de l'ambassade des Etats-Unis.

BULLETIN DU JOUR

La Délivrance

Mercredi, dans la soirée, le bruit se répandit que les Allemands étaient en train d'abandonner Lille. Hier, cette nouvelle se confirmait et, dans l'après-midi, tout le monde à Paris en était informé. Seuls les journaux, qui n'a jamais paru plus cruelle, devaient garder le silence de ne pouvoir clamer cette délivrance d'une partie du sol français, qui marquait une étape de plus dans la libération définitive de la patrie.

Plus heureuse que Saint-Quentin, que Cambrai, Lille, qui a vu ses tom-ber, est reconnaissable après la longue épreuve qu'elle a subie. Une population...

Comment les Alliés SONT ENTRÉS A LILLE

Une inoubliable Journée

Comme nous l'avons déjà dit, la prise de Lille, depuis quelques jours, ne faisait plus de doute pour personne ; depuis qua-rante-huit heures, la libération était ac-quise.

C'est dit-on, dans l'après-midi de mer-credi que des aviateurs anglais survolant la ville à faible hauteur, aperçurent des habitants qui, au moyen de linges, de vête-ments et de drapeaux leur faisaient des si-gnaux sur le caractère desquels il leur était impossible de se méprendre. Les Alle-mands avaient évacué Lille et en faisant sau-ter les ponts de la Deule et en fermant les portes.

Départ des derniers Allemands

Les aviateurs anglais s'empressèrent de faire rapport de ce qu'ils avaient vu à l'état-major de la 5e armée britannique, qui occu-pait les faubourgs sud-ouest de Lille de-puis comme plus du matin, que le lende-main, à cinq heures du matin, que les pre-miers soldats anglais purent entrer dans Lille par les portes de Canteleu et d'Isly.

Cependant qu'à peu près à la même heure la dernière patrouille allemande ayant franchi le pont-levis, fuyait dans la direction de Tournai par Fives et Hellemmes.

Cette première pénétration effectuée par quelques patrouilles isolées ne fut pas la véritable entrée qui n'eut lieu que le pré-midi, le commandement britannique ayant eu la pensée très chevaleresque d'attendre l'arrivée d'un bataillon de chasseurs à pied français, pour que nos compatriotes puissent prendre possession eux-mêmes de cité reconquise.

La grande nouvelle fut rapidement télé... à tous les états-majors des...

...régions envahies demandait qu'en cas d'armistice on imposât aux Allemands le rapatriement immédiat de tous nos compatriotes évacués en Belgique ou en Allemagne comme travailleurs civils, otages ou travailleurs prisonniers civils, sans distinction d'âge ni de sexe.

Cette mesure, le maréchal Foch l'im-posera comme un impitoyable sine qua non.

En attendant, la victoire vole de bef-froi en beffroi. Après Douai et Lille, nous aurons Roubaix et Tourcoing, vil-les sœurs de Lille. Bruges suivra Os-tende et Gand suivra Bruges.

L'heure de Dieu, c'est-à-dire l'heure de la Justice, va sonner. Il est moins cinq.

ALCESTE.

EMPRUNT DE LA LIBÉRATION

Apportez aux guichets de souscription :

Tous vos billets disponibles,

Vos dernières pièces d'or,

Et vos Bons de la Défense nationale !

30. — IMP. NAT.

(F) As we have already reported, the recapture of Lille has been doubted by no one for several days – for the last forty-eight hours the liberation has been assured.

It was on Wednesday afternoon, so it is said, that English airmen flying over the town at low altitude noticed some inhabitants who, by means of household linen, clothes and flags, were signalling to them in a fashion which it was impossible to misunderstand. The Germans had evacuated Lille, blowing up the bridges over the Deule, and closing the gates.

THE DEPARTURE OF THE LAST GERMANS

The English airmen hastened to report what they had seen to the staff officer of the British 5th Army, which was occupying the suburbs south-west of Lille, from Lomme as far as the Wattignies road via Loos and Haubourdin. Nevertheless, it was not until the next day at five in the morning, that the first English soldiers were able to enter Lille by the Cantelen and Isly gates, whilst at almost the same time the last German patrol, having cleared the Tournai gate and blown up the lift-bridge, were fleeing in the direction of Tournai, via Fives and Helennes.

This initial penetration, effected by a few isolated patrols, was not the real entry which did not take place until the afternoon, the British commander having conceived the very chivalrous notion of waiting for the arrival of a battalion of French light infantry, so that our compatriots could take possession themselves of the recaptured city ...

DELIVERANCE

... On Wednesday, in the evening, the word went round that the Germans were in the process of abandoning Lille. Yesterday this news was confirmed, and in the afternoon everyone in Paris knew of it. Only the newspapers, because of an inflexible rule which has never seemed more cruel, had to stay silent.

Ah – indubitably it pained us not to be able to shout the news of this deliverance of a part of the French soil, which marked another step forward in the complete liberation of the country.

Luckier than Saint-Quentin, than Cambrai, Lille, which has seen its chains fall off, is recognisable after the long trial which it has undergone. A section of the population was able to greet the victorious soldiers, and the invader, in his retreat, feeling punishment so close at hand and justice so resolute, did not smear its houses with tar for the torch of devastation.

It was saved, in that sense in which it is possible to be saved when the Germans have passed through; the walls remain, but the dwellings have been stripped of some of their furniture; the closed-up shops have seen their counters emptied, and in the deserted factories all the materials have disappeared. All that will be compensated for, and before long.

That is not all: before leaving, the *Bôches*, as if to recall the traditions of barbarian invaders, led away into captivity the men between fourteen and sixty years of age, having thrust whole families out onto the highways of exile. This is the last great crime for which reparation must be made as soon as possible.

Since yesterday the parliamentary group of the occupied regions have been demanding that in the event of an armistice the Germans should be forced to effect an immediate repatriation of all our compatriots who have been transported to Belgium or Germany as civilian prisoners, hostages or labourers, irrespective of age or sex. This measure will be imposed by Maréchal Foch as an unrelenting *sine qua non*.

Meanwhile, Victory flies from belfry to belfry. After Douai and Lille, we shall have Roubaix and Tourcoing, the sister towns to Lille. Bruges will follow Ostend, and Gand will follow Bruges.

God's hour, that is the hour of justice, is about to strike. It is five minutes to the hour.

ALCESTE

(translation of clippings opposite)

MABEL HAS FEW SOUVENIRS OF THE HISTORIC CEASE-FIRE AT 11 A.M. ON
NOVEMBER 11TH. SHE KEEPS A CUTTING OF GENERAL PÉTAIN'S ORDER OF
THE DAY INSTRUCTING CIVILISED BEHAVIOUR IN OCCUPIED TERRITORIES,
APPROVING OF ITS TONE
AND ALMOST BRITISH SENTIMENTS ...

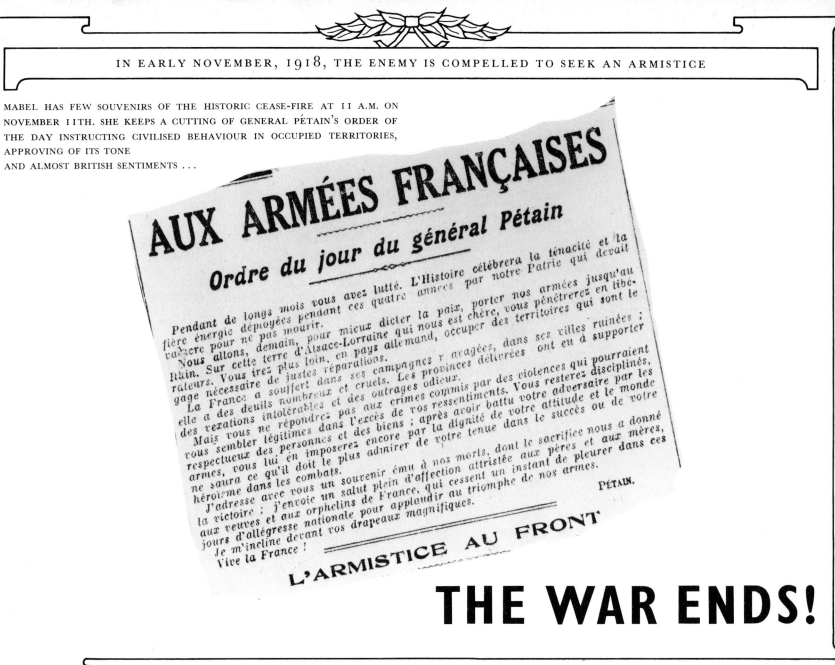

THE WAR ENDS!

For long months you have struggled. History will celebrate the tenacity and the rare energy displayed during these four years by our country, which had to win in order not to die.

We are going tomorrow, the better to dictate peace terms, to transport our armies to the Rhine. Into that land of Alsace-Lorraine, which is dear to us, you will enter as liberators. You will go still further into German lands, to occupy territories which are necessary forfeits of a just reparation.

France has suffered in its ravaged countryside, in its ruined towns; she has numerous and cruel bereavements. The liberated provinces have had to endure intolerable harassment and dreadful outrages.

But you will not respond to the crimes committed with acts of violence which might seem legitimate to you in the overflowing of your resentment. You will remain disciplined, respecting persons and goods; having beaten your adversary with arms, you will impress him still further by the dignity of your bearing, and the world will not know which to admire most: your conduct in victory, or your heroism in the fray.

I, with you, remember our dead, whose sacrifice has given us the victory. I send a greeting full of grieving affection to the fathers and mothers, to the widows and orphans of France, who cease weeping for a moment, in these days of national gladness, to applaud the triumph of our arms.

I bow before your magnificent battle colours.

Long live France!

PÉTAIN

(F)
Penvern en Treburden
November 12th, 1918

Dear Sister

We are still in Brittany, for an indefinite period, Château-Thierry having been very badly damaged by the *Bôches*, and our property there both dilapidated and ransacked. Your nice letters have, however, reached us, and my mother and I have had much pleasure in reading them. Please forgive us for not answering them sooner. One of my sisters came to spend the holiday months with us. She has connections in the district who visited us each day, so that what with my being at their disposal, and my mother wishing to afford them the most cordial hospitality, all our time was taken up.

Apart from that, we have had to think about completing our household arrangements here, with a view to staying through the winter, because the *Bôches* have so completely pillaged and broken up our Rue de la Madeleine house that we cannot think of living there, especially during the bad weather. My mother has much damage to complain of; two other houses of hers in different parts of the town are now no more than heaps of ruins, while another has one story missing. – The war and the Germans passed that way, dear Sister, and you know what that means. At last the end of all these horrors – the news of the Armistice has penetrated into this corner of Brittany, and has given rise to much popular rejoicing: but we do not know anything precise, the mail van having broken down, and we not having been able, because of that, to study the newspapers.

Well there must be no more fighting, that is essential. Brilliant victories by the Allies have brought about this fateful "*dénouement*", but one does not hope too much so soon. All my congratulations to your valiant English Army, which is covered with glory; we have now only to wish that our two countries will continue to bear for each other a precious feeling of friendship; that would make me doubly happy because of the great sympathy which exists between yourself and my mother and me.

N. Ponsin

25.11.18

Madelle. Weisweiler, with whom I worked, has asked me and Miss Wood, with the two Americans, to go down to her house on Thursday, in the Avenue Bois de Boulogne, to see the King pass; we are looking forward to a very exciting day.

Mab.

SOISSONS. — *Tour de la Cathédrale après le bombardement du 6 juillet 1915.*

MABEL GOES TO SEE THE KING PASS ...

November 29th, 1918 *(card not shown)*

Very many thanks for the box of sweets which arrived on Wednesday. We shall enjoy them very much indeed, and I am very pleased to be able to give some to the soldiers, who enjoy them immensely. Also thanks for paper yesterday. We saw the King, and watched the procession from a window in the Bois de Boulogne, yesterday, where Madelle. Weisweiler lives. Unfortunately it was a very wet day. Again many thanks and love to all.
   Mab.

... AND, AS ANOTHER YEAR DRAWS TO ITS CLOSE, SHE REVEALS A TRADE SECRET

10.12.18

Dearest Mother,
   Harry tells me what a dreadful cold you have; it is rather a long time since I heard from you, so am feeling rather anxious.
   Do you take quinine; it has always done me a lot of good; in fact all this year I have managed to keep off my colds with it. Am hoping soon to be coming home and shall then have to come back again just to finish.
   Heaps of love to you and Father from Mabel.

86 PONTOISE. — Notre Dame de Pontoise - Vierge miraculeuse — LL.

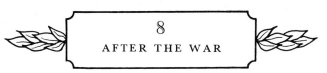

SHE AT FIRST WONDERS IF SHE IS STILL WANTED. A LETTER FROM A FRIEND AFFORDS SOME HOPE ...

(F) *(card not shown)*
Pontoise, December 29th, 1918

Dear Miss,

Your card which I received yesterday gave me great pleasure, as it did also to all your old patients who are still here. All have been very happy to have news of you and have charged me to tell you the great regret they felt in seeing you go; as you see there have not been any evacuations of patients since your departure. However, there have been further departures of nursing staff and we ask our-selves who will remain, and what the Red Cross is going to do with us. If this continues, the few wounded who are left with us will no longer have nurses.

I hope you are completely happy now you find yourself again at home. I wish you good health and all the best for 1919.

J. Bernard

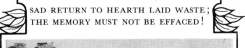

SAD RETURN TO HEARTH LAID WASTE; THE MEMORY MUST NOT BE EFFACED!

Nº 15 _ Triste retour au foyer dévasté... n'oubliez jamais! VISA Nº 1256

7.1.19

Dear Miss Jeff!

Latest news: A letter from Mrs. F.[1] today: granting *one week's extra leave* and saying that she is "waiting to hear from Miss Haswell before you and Sister Jeffery can return to France – as the *ambulances* close the Sisters are to return to England – I will write you as soon as I hear" – *Voilà!* – I think we may yet be going back to Pontoise. You and I together, love! – I should love it – even, as you say, though we seem not wanted! – especially as your patients are still there, poor things. Then – some-thing else – a letter from Mr. Wilkins this morning asking for photos – signatures etc. in connection with passport! Things are beginning to buzz in *that* corner at any rate. Meantime we sit tight and wait for Mrs. F.'s next letter. – I shall hardly be able to open it with excitement. Much love from your old *camarade* – letter from Grillon today. No work for her in Strasbourg. She is asking for *more* leave and is then going to the Pyrenees.

F. A. H. Wood.

1. Mrs. Ethel G. Fenwick, director of the French Flag Nursing Corps and Secretary of the British Committee of the French Red Cross. She was married to Bedford Fenwick, the Senior Gynaecologist to the Hospital for Women, Soho.

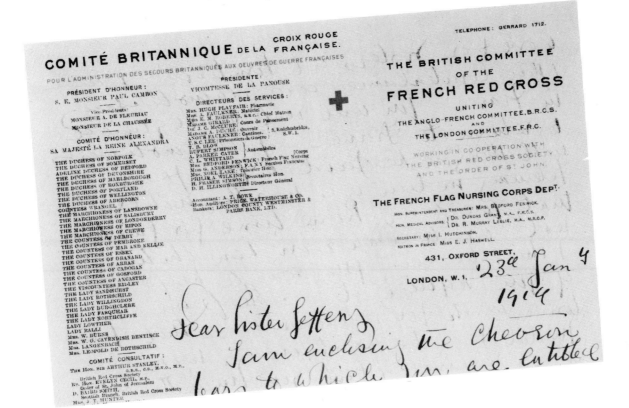

January 23rd, 1919

Dear Sister Jeffery,

I am enclosing the chevron bars to which you are entitled for 2½ years service in France – time spent on leave is deducted – the wide bar is for first year, and the three narrow for subsequent six months – as the bars are blue and will not show on a blue coat, I am enclosing a piece of ribbon on which they can be mounted. As it appears there is no further work for Sisters at Pontoise – and all other *Ambulances* are demobilising in France, you will not be required to return to France – full emoluments will therefore be paid to you for February in lieu of a months notice, so that you will have time for further rest, – or to enter on new duties –

I shall be very pleased to help you if you require it – keep me in touch with your address so that your medal may be sent on as soon as it is received, but you know the French are not very quick about such things – I hope you will not be very disappointed at not returning to France, and you will later receive some form of thanks from the Comité Britannique for your excellent services. With very kind regards

I remain

Yours very truly, Ethel G. Fenwick

La Guerre 1914-19
L. C. H. Paris

871. Château-Thiéry (Aisne) -- Quai Fausse Marne

CHÂTEAU-THIERRY – AT THE OLD CHÂTEAU –
THE MARNE VALLEY AND ST. CREPIN'S TOWER

Cité Paris 2939

Ehrhard, phot., Château-Thierry

491 CHÂTEAU-THIERRY. — Sur le Vieux Château - Vallée de la Marne et Tour St-Crepin

(undated card to Mabel)

Have just had news that my Mother has been very ill in bed for a week with Grippe! I was so sorry to be rushed off in such a hurry. Then when I got to Paris, found *less* need for hurry. Am working in the neighbourhood of the Courcelles battlefield, not far from Montdidier but a long way off Davenecourt where Mme. Panas and Co. are. – Have you any news!? Hope you will come out. – Feel sure you will! – Do let me know if you do! I am only temporary here, until the Sister who is ill, returns. Much love dear *old Chum*
   from yours ever Adine Wood

(card to Mabel)

My dear old Jeff!
I feel most dreadfully guilty and sorry for not having written you that long letter yet! My thoughts often fly to you. I had the greatest good luck on Easter Monday to go by motor to Château-Thierry via Compiègne and Soissons. Poor old Soissons – so different to the day we went together. – Cathedral in ruins. – Wished you had been with me. – I was sorry not to go to Vauxbuin, was told there was not time. We are frantically busy. Will really write you account of work as soon as I can get time to myself, – which is *rare*.
   F.A.H. Wood April 29th, 1919

SERBIA AND THE FIRST WORLD WAR

The First World War was essentially a war of great powers; among the small powers involved were two Slavic countries: Bulgaria, and Serbia whose cause in a sense started the war. Bulgaria's ruler was a Teuton sympathetic to Austria-Hungary and to Germany. Serbia's ruler was a Slav, King Peter, who had successfully warred against Bulgaria in 1913. Serbian independence inspired unrest among other Slavic domains ruled by Austria-Hungary, such as Bosnia and Hercegovina. For this and other reasons, many Austrians wanted an excuse to invade Serbia.

Such an excuse arose when the Archduke Franz Ferdinand, heir to the Austrian throne, was shot by a young Bosnian, Gavrilo Princip, on June 28th, 1914, while on a visit to the Bosnian town and Austro-Hungarian regional centre, Sarajevo. Serbia had warned the unpopular Archduke against this visit, and Austrian investigators later found no evidence to blame the Serbian government for this crime with which, however, some Serbian reactionaries were involved through providing arms to Bosnian insurgents. Indeed, Austrian protection of the Archduke had been so inadequate as to suggest that some war-mongering Austrians may have wished this event to occur, since the Archduke was also far from popular in Austria. Serbia was, however, blamed and soon invaded by Austria, starting the chain of events which brought the rest of Europe into the war.

The initial attack on Belgrade in the summer of 1914 was valiantly repulsed by Serbian forces who were, however, at a low ebb through continual fighting since 1912; first along with Montenegro, Greece, Romania and Bulgaria against the Turks who were finally expelled from Macedonia, and then against Bulgaria about who owned Macedonia afterwards. Typhus raged in Serbia in the winter of 1914 and further ravaged the army. When the Austrians returned in 1915 with Bulgarian support, Belgrade was captured and by November the fatigued Serbian army was driven south to Kosovo plain, a position east of Montenegro and Albania which was cut off from the support of French and English armies gathering in northern Greece, around Salonika.

Snow enveloped Kosovo plain and the Serbians realised that they could not sustain a prolonged fight. They decided to retreat from their country in order to make a fighting return when they could. But the enemy had cut off all but one possible escape route. This lay across the perilous mountains of Albania and Montenegro, through territories sympathetic to Austria where the Serbians could not hope for provisioning. A medical unit of the Scottish Women's Suffrage Federation accompanied the army on this harsh retreat where hunger, cold, Albanian sniping and renewed typhus claimed many thousands of lives. The survivors, around 155,000 men, were evacuated to the Greek island of Corfu where they rested sufficiently to return via Salonika next year, triumphantly defeating Bulgarians and Germans in the difficult battle of Kajmak-čelan, or the butter-tub peak, in Macedonia in November, 1916. Bulgaria then withdrew from the war and the Serbian army sparred with the remaining enemy in Macedonia until the arrival of Allied troops enabled them to liberate the rest of Serbia in the autumn of 1918. The war cost Serbia around one-half of its total population. Serbia gained by the war other Slav-speaking regions taken from Austria, forming the present-day land of the South Slavs, or Yugoslavia. [M. W.]

to Mrs. Adeline Jeffery, 57 Redcar Rd., Sheffield   18.8.19

This shows you just a bit of the mountains – much better than my drawing. There are not many picture postcards about yet, but will send you all I see. How is the "spot"?[1]

1. Who or what "the spot" was, remains obscure.

VRANJE — CONFECTIONERS
This card was produced to be used by the occupying Austrian army.

Vranje   Zuckerwarenhändler

to H. Jeffery, Esq.[2]—23.9.19   M. E. Jeffery, Sister – Belgrade

Please thank Mother for her last letter of September 11th. Am glad the weather has improved and the garden so flourishing. Do you like these p.p.cs.? W.B.L.

2. Some Yugoslav historians conclude that, by an amazing mistake, this postcard (sent to Mabel's brother Harry) does not represent King Peter, but rather Vojvode Putnik (1847–1917), Field Marshal and Chief of Staff of the Serbian army until his death. Others demonstrate that King Peter grew this unfamiliar double beard on Corfu, and is so shown in a recently published photograph dating from his time on Corfu. Vojvode Putnik's beard was somewhat different.

ПЕТАР I. *PETER. I.*
PETAK
Крал. Срба, Хрвата и Словенаца
KRALI SRBA,   *King of Serbs*

110

"DO YOU LIKE THESE P.P.CS.?"

The following three postcards appeared in a series called "In the War for Freedom 1914–18". All the photographs were taken by a Serbian army priest, Šuković.

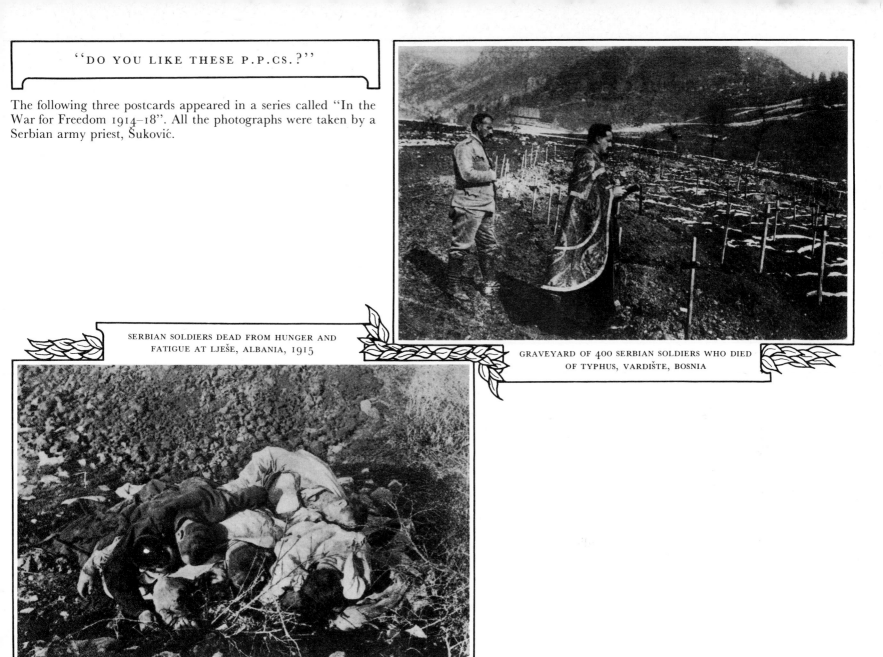

SERBIAN SOLDIERS DEAD FROM HUNGER AND
FATIGUE AT LJEŠE, ALBANIA, 1915

GRAVEYARD OF 400 SERBIAN SOLDIERS WHO DIED
OF TYPHUS, VARDIŠTE, BOSNIA

"A little Corporal age 10 – reporting that his parents have been killed" (*Mabel's explanation of the Serbian on reverse*: Corporal Momčilo Gavrić of 10 years, volunteer whose parents were killed by Austrian soldiers, arrives with his comrade to report to officers.)

CORPORAL MOMČILO GAVRIĆ OF 10 YEARS

THE ARRIVAL OF THE SERBIAN ARMY AT CORFU

S.W.H.
Belgrade
27.9.19

Many thanks for envelopes received today. W.B.L. Mab.

MABEL IS STRANDED WITHOUT HER SEWING BAG ...

Scottish Women's Hospitals, Belgrade
2.10.19

O.A.S.

Many thanks for paper yesterday and letter today of September 20. Am glad you liked the present. Have just sent a card to Jim at Athens, sorry he does not pass this way. Please send me a little wool (black and white) in a letter.

Mine has all gone with the bag.

M. E. Jeffery
Sister

(*Mabel on reverse:*) "Battlefield of – after one year"

THE BATTLEFIELD OF KAJMAK-ČELAN
AFTER A YEAR HAD PASSED

AUSTRIAN "CULTURE" AND "JUSTICE":
THE HANGING OF SERBS IN HERCEGOVINA[1]

10.10.19

Many thanks for Father's letter yesterday. Please send me a few more envelopes for p.cs. They seem to say we are all coming home soon but nothing is quite settled yet, except that we cannot go back to the hospital at Vranje, as the place is now full of soldiers. It has turned colder but I still only wear one garment very thin, underneath the overall. They have given me cotton, buttons, tape, to replace a little what was lost.

Love to all. Hope "Rosie" is quite well – does she still smile?[2]

Kiss to Rene and the new dolly.

Mabel

1. Reprisals after the Archduke Franz Ferdinand's assassination.
2. Rosie was the old dolly.

4.11.19

Dear Baby,
This is a picture of some nice gardens like those where you go sometimes with Grandpa.
You see there is a tiny baby going for a walk.

I shall bring you a present when I come home – perhaps a dolly or some cups and saucers, and we can go for a walk in the park with your white umbrella. Bonjour.
A big kiss from
Auntie Mabel

Scottish Women's Hospitals, Belgrade 1920.
Group including Dr. Emslie[1]

BELGRADE, KALIMEGDAN PARK

БЕОГРАД. — BEOGRAD. Kalimegdan.

Snow picnic at Topčidar Park, Belgrade 1920.
Group including Dr. Emslie and Dr. Mackenzie.

1. Later Lady I. E. Hutton, author of *With a Women's Unit in Serbia*, London 1928. She supervised the move of numerous wounded from Salonika to Vranje after the Armistice in 1918.

MONTENEGRIN WOMEN CARRYING
ARMY EQUIPMENT

Dearest Daddy,   13.2.20
Many thanks for yours today with card from the French Red Cross. When they see my length of service, without any decoration, perhaps they will think also to send me a medal! This is very like the mountain roads at Vranje, except that the cliffs are not so steep or bare; we used to go and bathe in the pools up the ravines.

The churches are very "Eastern"; the Dalmatian soldier who looked after us from Belgrade said that the Bulgars used to fill them with civilians and then blow them up. Most of the houses along the railway – especially the stations – are all wrecked, but they are gradually building them up and the names are written in English letters as well as the others. Dr. Emslie has gone to Constantinople.

Thanks for letter sent on.   Love to all, Mabel.

S.W.H.
April 15th, 1920

Dear Harry,
Many thanks for yours, with labels. The letter with lists of trains has not arrived yet. Am thinking I may be home before this but am staying a few days in France.

M. Jeffery

(*French subtitle to postcard*)
The King did not want official recognition, but all the length of the road people were waiting to receive their old sovereign from exile.

THE RETURN OF KING PETER INTO SERBIA

LA RENTRÉE DU ROI PIERRE EN SERBIE
ПОВРАТАК КРАЉА ПЕТРА У СРБИЈУ.

TECHNICAL SCHOOL, RHEIMS

10 - REIMS (1919) - Rue de Talleyrand - Ecole Industrielle
Talleyrand Street   Industrious School

Vue prise avec objectif Hermagis

La Dispensaire
Baraquement 30
rue du Châlet, Rheims
Showing the *barraques* – ours is the next one down the road.
You can imagine the mud when it was about 5 ft. deeper across
the road.

WAR DEAD UNBURIED.

12,500 French Soldiers in Big Shed.

(BY ARRANGEMENT WITH "THE TIMES," LONDON.)

PARIS, Friday.

The newspaper, "Paris-Soir," published yesterday a message from a special correspondent at Verdun which declared that the bodies of 12,500 French soldiers were lying at Douaumont unburied in rough wooden boxes not even nailed down and seven men to a box. Of these, it is stated 9,800 have lain in a big shed for six years.

In conversation to-day, M. Champetier de Ribes, Minister of Pensions, said that, unfortunately the message was correct in substance.—Per Press Association (copyright).

An old trench at Verdun. All separate bones are now collected and put in coffins labelled according to the "*secteur*" where they are found; and put in the chapel at the old fort at Douaumont – where there is an old army priest – (decorated) always in attendance. (*Mabel on reverse*)

THE DEFENCE OF VERDUN — THE RAVINE OF THE DEAD — A TRENCH

La Défense de Verdun — Le Ravin de la Mort - Une tranchée.

Le Front de Champagne ? — Massif de MORONVILLIERS
"Le Casque" Célèbre par les Combats d'Avril 1917

100. — La Grande Guerre (ses Ruines). — PLATEAU DE CRAONNE. — Le Cimetière.

Thuillier, éditeur - Epernay.

101. — La Grande Guerre (ses Ruines). — PLATEAU DE CRAONNE. — Un Abri blindé.

664 LES RUINES DE LA GRANDE GUERRE. - Tranchées allemandes au Défilé des Cavaliers de Courcy
Great War Ruins — German's trenches at Courcy — LL

Ruines des environs d'Ypres 1914-18 Cimetière anglais dans un bois.
The ruins near Ypres English cemetery in a wood.

Ruines d'Ypres 1914-18 Caserne.
The ruins of Ypres The barracks.

Visé Paris n° 696 696 LES RUINES DE LA GRANDE GUERRE. — Proyart. — Poste d'ambulance.
Great War Ruins. — Proyart. — Field hospital. — LL.

71 Verdun — Fort de Vaux, au premier plan, tombe de soldat français
Fortress of Vaux a French soldier tomb

Blampey Bros
MEDALLISTS
Artists in oil & water colours
106 UPPER STREET 106
ISLINGTON London, N.

"And when we come to the end of life the only things that seem worth while our having done, are the sacrifices we have made for others." (*A final entry in Mabel's notebooks, made about the time of this photograph*)

Yes, well, we've been through another war since then. That was supposed to be the war to end all wars, but you can see what a fat lot of good it did.

I think Auntie Mabel brought some very peculiar things home. All war mementos. I suppose that would have been the thing, wouldn't it. They're all over the house. There's one even stuck in the tree there, feeding the birds. Well I reckon I've got them to better use. I can't think how she got them all home; they were all brass, and heavy.

I keep Auntie Mabel's bowl like a bomb in the kitchen.[1] It was very banged and battered, because it's rather roly-poly and apt to roll around. And that top part there was badly stained. It's not brass, but some kind of metal. And I decided not to fiddle or fume around so I painted it with gold paint. And Jack and Joe took it up to the workshop. It had a lot of roly-poly bumps, but it's a whole lot better now than it was before. I can remember it in Moor Cliff, in Granny's house. It used to have sweeties in it, in the sideboard. That was an attraction. But it's a pretty gruesome reminder, isn't it?

Don't you think her mother would have preferred a nice little piece of lace?

1. This object was made in imitation of the flaming bomb device used as a badge by the infantries of most European nations. It appeared on the front of the French infantryman's steel helmet. [M. W., J. C.]

Now that silk bag. I found it in the bottom of the side-board drawer, and I suppose it's been there ever since it was given to mother, because it doesn't look as if she ever used it, does it. And now it's all over brown marks! I *imagine* it was given to mother; I really don't know any history about it at all. But seeing it's got Amiens on the back, I imagine it came from Auntie Mabel at some time. Seems rather different from her taste in shell cases, wouldn't you say?

You know Auntie Mabel took quite an interest in British royalty. Like lots of people brought up in Victorian times she had this Empire thing. And she had a tin box we've got for receipts somewhere, and you can hardly see the picture on it. But it's something to do with Queen Victoria – probably the coronation.[1] So she took this tin to a little antique shop and asked the man did he think Queen Mary would like to have it, because it was about her relative. And I thought what a funny thing to do; it was only an old tin can. Queen Mary would have had priceless things. But to Victorian families, the royal family was quite a thing, and in some funny way, they had a kind of personal allegiance to them. And I suppose that was why she thought Queen Mary would have liked that tin. But really and truly – I ask you – with all the treasures Queen Mary had! Still, Auntie Mabel did these unusual things sometimes.

1. An example of this tin, in excellent condition, is in the collection of Colman Foods, Carrow, Norwich. The tin was issued in connection with the Diamond Jubilee of Queen Victoria on June 22nd, 1897. The picture on the lid is of the coronation ceremony in Westminster Abbey on June 22nd, 1838, and the procession is probably that which took place for the opening of the Imperial Institute, May 10th, 1893. We are grateful to R. H. Butcher of Colman Foods for this information. [M. W., J. C.]

That picture would be about 1952. She looks quite sad doesn't she. Auntie Mabel's mother started to get frail in the mid-20s, and in 1929 she had a really bad stroke, and from then on was nursed by Mabel almost single-handed round that big Victorian house, Moor Cliff, and her father would have needed looking after too. He died in 1935 or 1936; Granny died in 1931. For two years before she had been paralysed and nearly blind, and Auntie Mabel nursed her completely. They had only the one maid, Evie, at Moor Cliff, and Mabel did her nursing upstairs. I suppose nowadays with hospitals so much improved they'd have made arrangements in one; you need strong arms for these heavy cases.

I don't know how she managed single-handed but she did. She must have had terrific guts. Funny the story of people's lives!

Then Auntie Mabel was left Moor Cliff, and had to pay bills on it, which I guess left her pocket cleared out. And it was built some time near the end of the century and they don't last forever, these houses. They're always needing something, even if it's only paint.

Then she took herself to the east coast of England, for a reason nobody knows. It was the very devil to get there. She died in 1957 or 1958.

And the last thing I heard of the house was when the solicitor said, "Your Auntie Mabel planned to leave you Moor Cliff", and I was very elated. But in the next breath he said, "But she changed her mind and now it's part of Sheffield University."

A POEM BY AUNTIE MABEL

Tear up the old reminders
Of days that are past and gone,
For soon in the glow of the evening
We shall face the western sun,
And come again with our loved ones,
With those who have gone away.
And then, in a brighter morning,
Enjoy another day.

Oh look, here's just one more photograph I found, of Auntie Mabel, Grandpa and me.

That was taken on the sands at Scarborough, and mine wouldn't go. Until two sailor boys came along and rattled a money box behind him; then he just *fled*, and I was hanging on with my arms round his neck!

Grandpa with his hat on backwards and him backwards! Aren't donkeys gorgeous. I think they're priceless. I think they have such appealing little faces.

THE END

The idea of a league of Red Cross Societies was conceived through the inspiration of a Swiss national, Henri Dunant, who observed the plight of those affected by the Battle of San Solferino in North Italy in June, 1859. He saw the need for an international relief organisation, politically neutral, which would care for both soldiers and civilians in time of war. This would be to augment the efforts of inadequate military medical services and of the Church, which had looked after the wounded and destitute since the Middle Ages. Individual relief societies were to be organised nationally, but it was agreed that all of them would follow rules decided upon by an international conference, the first of which met in Geneva in October, 1863.

The basic principles adopted at the first Geneva Convention were:
– The setting up in each country of a Relief Committee capable of assisting the Army Medical Services in wartime
– the training of voluntary nurses in peacetime
– the neutralisation of ambulances, military hospitals and medical personnel
– the adoption of a uniform and distinctive emblem, a white arm band with a red cross.

The Geneva Convention provisions were augmented in a succession of conferences held throughout the past century; it was intended that each member country of the League of Red Cross Societies should prepare itself in peacetime for the eventuality of war. In 1909 the British Red Cross Society organised their Voluntary Aid Scheme. Numerous Voluntary Aid Detachments, whence comes the abbreviation V.A.D., were set up throughout Britain, consisting of men and women volunteers to be trained in first aid and nursing. In peacetime they assisted local hospitals, or the territorial army on manœuvres. On the outbreak of the First World War many Voluntary Aid Detachment members were sent to assist in hospitals abroad, particularly as ambulance drivers, kitchen assistants and nurses' aids. V.A.D.s working as general hospital help can be recognised in Auntie Mabel's Royaumont photographs by their distinctive ruffled caps (p. 27).

V.A.D.s were Red Cross personnel from the time of their initial volunteering, whilst many trained nurses, like Mabel Jeffery, who were not in peacetime members of the Red Cross came under its control for wartime service after enlisting. Also in wartime many private medical relief organisations had their activities coordinated by the Red Cross.

Both organisations with which Mabel Jeffery worked during the war, the Scottish Women's Hospitals and the French Flag Nursing Corps, were represented on the British Committee of the French Red Cross, under whose auspices they operated in France. Auntie Mabel herself was never a member of the British Red Cross.

Elsie Maud Inglis was born in India in 1864, her father being an East India Company employee there. Her childhood was spent in India, but on her father's retirement in 1878 the family settled in Edinburgh. Elsie Inglis determined to enter the medical profession at a time when there was still much opposition to women in that field; and, once qualified, she herself did much to ameliorate the situation for women doctors in Scotland, being instrumental in setting up a medical school for women and also a maternity hospital staffed by women, who were at that time excluded from resident posts in the chief Edinburgh hospitals. She held various surgical appointments, and also practised privately.

At the turn of the century Elsie Inglis became involved in the feminist movement. She gave lectures under the wing of Mrs. Fawcett's group, and in 1906 founded the Scottish Women's Suffrage Society. Feminism in Scotland grew strong, as elsewhere, and it was at a committee meeting of the Scottish Women's Suffrage Federation, in August, 1914, that the idea of a Scottish Women's Hospitals Committee was put forward. The object was to provide hospital units to serve in Europe, where war had just broken out, and the idea having been adopted, Elsie Inglis toured the country fund- and staff-raising. So successful was she that the first unit was sent out to France in November, 1914, where several hospitals were set up (see the account on p. 26), and a second unit went out to Serbia in January, 1915.

After organising several more medical units, Elsie Inglis herself went to Serbia in April, 1915, to replace a doctor who had contracted a severe illness, and arriving just as the typhus epidemic had subsided was able to devote herself to establishing three hospitals in the north of the country, in anticipation of extensive fighting in the autumn.

When the German, Austrian and Bulgarian armies invaded Serbia in the autumn of 1915 these three hospitals had to be rapidly evacuated, as, a little later, did the hospitals further south to which the patients were transferred. The enemy advanced inexorably, and rather than constantly retreating Elsie Inglis decided to stay in Kruševac; and her team went on working there for some months after the Germans and Austrians had taken the town in November. At the end of this time most of the patients were transferred to Hungary, and Elsie Inglis and her unit were taken under guard to Belgrade and on to Vienna, where, owing to the intervention of the American diplomatic staff, they were set free and allowed to return to Britain. Meanwhile another Scottish Women's Hospitals unit in Serbia continued with the retreating troops (see p. 109).

Back home Elsie Inglis failed to interest the War Office in her scheme for sending a medical unit to Mesopotamia, but was able, after a brief visit of inspection to the Corsica unit, to organise two teams to work with the Serbian division in Russia, at the request of the Serbs. She went to Russia in August, 1916, and her units worked first with the Serbian division, then with the Russians while the Serbs were re-forming after disastrous losses. The unit stayed with the Russians until August, 1917, despite difficulties created by the revolution, then returned to help the Serbs, whose position in Russia was now unsafe because of the changes in Russian policy towards the war. Elsie Inglis refused to withdraw, despite entreaties from home, until the Serbs had been safely evacuated.

Her health was now deteriorating fast, and when the unit returned to Britain in November, 1917, she was very ill. She died soon after landing at Newcastle, her last wishes being that her committee continue to do all possible to help the Serbs, which indeed it did, sending units back to the reconquered country which stayed on after war ended (see p. 109).

The Scottish Women's Hospitals Committee was a product of the movement for the political enfranchisement of women, and of the conditions of the war in Europe. Its work was accomplished when women won the vote and when the aftermath of the war had been dealt with as far as the capacity of the S.W.H. allowed; but if Elsie Inglis, its guiding spirit, is perhaps little remembered in Britain despite several hospital wards bearing her name, her memory is revered to this day in Yugoslavia, where the Serbian people have never forgotten the heroism of her units during their struggle for survival. An Elsie Inglis Memorial Hospital was opened in Belgrade in 1929. It remained in use until it was amalgamated with two other hospitals in recent years.